Super
Living Rooms

Super Living Rooms

Emily Malino

Illustrations by Sally Andrews

Random House New York

Library of Congress Cataloging in Publication Data
Malino, Emily.
Super living rooms.

1. House furnishings. 2. Interior decoration.
3. Living rooms. I. Title.
TX311.M26   747'.75   75–40558
ISBN 0–394–49901–8
ISBN 0–394–73103–4 pbk.

Manufactured in the United States of America
98765432
First Edition

To my helpful and patient family which includes Jim,
Laurie, Betsy, Jamie and John, plus Lucy and even Misty,
I dedicate this book with love. They gave, I took,
and I hope this book is worth their generosity.

ACKNOWLEDGMENTS

I could never have begun or completed this book
without the constant nudging of Steve Martindale,
the willing assistance of Pam Radford and Sally Vogt,
the gentle corrections of my editors and the major
contributions of all my clients, past and present, whose
many problems I have attempted to solve herein.

Contents

Introduction

Many designers make it sound as if decorating is as easy as falling off a log. Then, after that disclaimer, they proceed to show you pictures of gorgeous rooms that only a professional could design.

The truth is that decorating, especially a "public room" like the living room, is *not* easy, but it is possible. The reason so many people cannot achieve the living room of their dreams is that the room is, indeed, a dream. It is unrealistic, something seen, perhaps, in a photograph and unattainable within the budget and design experience you bring to the job. Be realistic; plan a room that reflects your needs, not your neighbors' needs or the needs of some anonymous family in a slick magazine.

Let me tell you a secret. Many of the rooms that you see in magazines are not real at all; they are set up in empty rooms in a home or apartment, or even in a photographer's studio, with furniture borrowed from a manufacturer. Real interior designers design the space and place the furniture, but it is only a model, or a temporary display, geared solely for publication. There is nothing illegal about this procedure; I've designed these make-believe spaces myself. It is simply that they can be misleading, often unreal and occasionally downright impractical, but then, you see, no one lives there, so it doesn't matter.

You live in your home, and your living room should be a reflection of your own tastes, your own interests, your own hobbies. If you have a family, the room should accommodate all its members instead of being a place where only guests feel at home. The furniture must be versatile enough to suit many needs; the surfaces should be practical so that you will not be apprehensive if your fifteen-year-old son decides to do his homework on the coffee table or if a visitor brings a very young child along. The furniture arrangement should be as efficient for social gatherings as for a solitary reader, as satisfying to the bridge player's foursome as to the teenager listening to music or to you writing a letter or paying bills at your desk. All of these and many more can be built into the capacity of even the smallest living room, if you once accept the idea that this is not a room only for looking but for living.

Living should be a pleasure and designing your own room should give you pleasure as well. It need not be a frightening or demoralizing experience, and it won't necessarily cost an arm and a leg if you use common sense and the imagination you were born with. These are the two basic ingredients of a successful room.

If you were to stop and analyze a room that appeals to you, whether in the flesh or in a magazine, you would see that common-sense ideas of furniture size, arrangement, color and pattern prevail in a kind of subtle logic that makes everything seem right. Remember that the various parts of any room can be divided into three categories: forms—the furniture in the room; backgrounds—the walls, windows and floors; and accents—the lighting and accessories.

Imagination is something else: this is the added touch that makes the room different and unusual. And who can do this better than you, the dweller, the lucky man or woman who will be using this splendid space, this mini-palace of your own?

Let's put it in business terms: you are the decorator and the client as well. This is an enviable merger because you can analyze and estimate and budget with far greater experience than two total strangers meeting for the first time could ever accomplish. As for know-how, well, I am going to teach you how to analyze your own needs and convert these into a room for living that will please you, please your family and delight your guests.

Super
Living Rooms

Who Are You?

Before you begin decorating your living room, you ought to have some ideas about the answer to that question. Don't worry, you don't have to add the cost of psychoanalysis to the cost of your new couch, but it is amazing how much your psyche is involved in decorating your home. It used to be the eyes, but in our time, it is the home—and especially the living room—which many people consider "the mirror of the soul." Our clothes are important in helping us project our physical self and bolster our psyche by making us feel more self-confident. Our car is sometimes an expression of our psyche, a moving symbol which defines our status and position. But our home is much more than these. Though it may show how successful we are financially and help make us feel secure and easy with visitors, our home should be more than a display of financial success; it should be a reflection of our intellect and our interests, our inner selves, our lifestyle.

A hundred or more years ago, most people lived in similar single-family homes in thousands of towns all across the country. Today people live in high-rise apartment towers in the middle of large urban centers; they live in townhouse clusters at the edges of big cities; they live in mobile-home communities; and they still live in single-family homes in the country and the suburbs. Many of these habitations would have seemed alien to our great-grandparents, but it is this very variety that makes it possible for you to choose the particular way you want to live. Before you begin to think about your living room, analyze your lifestyle and see how it will affect the look and use of your home. More than any other effort, designing your home involves all of you—

1

your psyche, your interests, your talent and your potential. Moreover, it also involves your family; they should be a part of the process so that their needs are also reflected in the final result.

Think of living rooms you have liked. Try to figure out what you like specifically about them and how these special effects would fit you, your family and your lifestyle.

Your Lifestyle Questionnaire

The first step in designing your living room is to explore *how* others live and how you live; the second step is to decide on *what* goes into the room. The "how" coming ahead of the "what" may be a new approach; a lot of rooms I have seen look as though the what came first, as though the owner saw something in a store, bought it and then tried to find a place for it in his or her home. Haven't you tried that approach and found that it rarely works? How often have you regretted a purchase and wished you had waited to see if it worked before plunking down your money? Impulse buying is a human failing that even "specialists" like me sometimes succumb to.

To avoid such mistakes, it is helpful to follow the same formula that most interior designers use. In interviews with clients, long before they put pencil to paper, they develop a set of simple questions that must be answered before any design work is started. I have outlined this kind of questionnaire for you, and it will help you to get a professional perspective on your lifestyle and will influence the plans and decisions you make in your living room.

DESIGNER'S QUESTIONNAIRE

Family Facts

1. Are you married or single?

2. Children?

Female	How many	Ages
Male	How many	Ages

3. Pets

Dogs	How many	Large or small
Cats	How many	Large or small
Other	How many	Large or small

How Do You Use the Room?

1. Do you entertain in your living room?
   Often
   Occasionally
   Infrequently

2. Do you like to have
   Big parties
   Small parties

3. Is your style of entertaining
   Formal
   Informal

4. Do you dine in your living room? If so, is this dining area in daily use or just for parties?

5. Do you use your living room for hobbies or working? What daily activities like watching television or playing games or listening to music go on in your living room?

What Are the Existing Physical Characteristics of the Room?

1. What kind of windows do you have?
   Large picture window
   Separated small windows
   Bow or bay window
   Doors to garden or outdoors
   Any combination of the above

2. Do you have a view you like?

3. Do you need privacy at the windows? Light control?

4. What kind of floors do you have?

Wood	Good condition	
	Needs refinishing	
Carpet	Good condition	Color
	Need new carpet	
Area rug	You like	
	You want to buy	

5. What kind of walls do you have?

Dry wall	Painted	Color
	Needs repainting or other finish	
Paneling	Too dark	Color
Papered walls	Pattern	Predominant colors
	Needs repapering	Background color
	Would like to paint instead	

Personal Preferences

1. What kind of art do you have or do you want?
   A collection of

   Small framed prints, paintings, drawings

   Small objets d'art

   One large painting, print or poster

   One or two medium-sized paintings, prints or posters

   Sculpture

   Small

   Medium

   Large

2. Do you have or want plants?
   Table-based potted plants
   Tree-sized potted plants
   A planting area

3. Do you want a particular style?

4. Do you prefer formal or informal rooms?

Family Facts

Married or Single?

Begin your lifestyle analysis with yourself and your family. Whether you are married or single obviously makes an enormous difference. If you're married you have to share the existing space and fit the needs, interests and preferences of two people together into a cohesive room. This isn't always as easy as it sounds. Many interior designers I know claim they are practicing psychiatrists because each session with husband and wife sounds like an encounter group. Some couples have never actually explored their needs and taste preferences in design, and the designer is helping them realize how much they agree or disagree on a fundamental approach to space—and to their life together.

How About Children?

Children come next. People who don't live with children cannot possibly realize how different a family living room must be from a room used only by adults. After all, there is no reason why a perfectly attractive and stylish room cannot suit children as well as grownups. On the other hand, common sense must prevail; don't choose a soft suede leather upholstery that buttery fingers can permanently mark; don't choose a white silk that will soon be polka-dotted with chocolate Oreo stains. A good idea is to have a child's chair as well as grownups' chairs. They can be a handsome addition to the room, especially if you find an old one with character.

If you have older teenage children, don't buy expensive fragile antique furniture. Make sure to arrange your room with a big coffee table; teens like to have a place for feet as well as peanut butter sandwiches, soda and pizza. My advice to you is to plan with children in mind all the way; if you don't, you will be in a constant state of panic whenever someone under twenty-one uses your living room.

Pets Make a Difference

Pets are something else. Unless you're a pet freak, I don't see why a non-house-trained animal cannot be kept out of the parlor, if necessary with a pair of doors to block the entrance or, barring doors, a loud voice and rolled-up newspaper. I designed a living room for a family with two big boxer dogs; they were house-trained but so bouncy that just wiggling their rear ends in boxer joy made them impossible living room visitors—not to mention their primeval need to join people on sofas and chairs. I had a pair of wooden doors made in a geometric sculpted Moorish design, hinged to meet in the middle with a latch, and finished them in the same rich dark color as the wood floors. They are a splendid addition to the room, keeping the dogs out while letting light in, and they can be draped with a sheet on Christmas morning to keep small people from seeing what Santa left, at least until after breakfast.

How Do You Use Your Living Room?

The next step is to ask yourself how you plan to use the room. If your interests are as diverse as most people's, you will want your living room to be versatile, to serve several needs, and yet have a look that pleases you.

Entertaining

One of the most important questions to ask is how often you entertain, whether you like big or small groups and how you plan to wine and dine these guests. I think you'll agree that there could be a vast visual difference between a household that has the habit of having one or two couples over for a quiet evening and the one that goes in for big bashes for cocktails.

For the former, sensible people, the normal seating group will be perfectly adequate. A sofa and two easy chairs can seat four or five comfortably, and an occasional chair or two can always be brought over from a corner or from the dining table. My guideline is to have enough space for six to be seated comfortably without moving furniture. This is almost always possible, even in the smallest room.

For those of you who do have tiny rooms and doubt my word, go to your nearest library and check out any book on Scandinavian design; you will see that these clever people, many of whom live in much smaller homes than ours, have been able to think through their space and people problems and come to a simple answer: lightweight and easily moved furniture.

I've worked on rooms that looked too small to squeeze in anything more than a chair and table, but which I was able to stretch to contain a perfectly adequate seating group. Be brave and unconventional. If your room is small, stay away from overstuffed upholstery; try a small sofa and two open-arm chairs, with a glass-topped coffee table between them and two occasional cane seat-and-back armchairs to pull over for extras. In one tiny room I worked on there wasn't room for a sofa at all, so I settled for four nice large barrel-shaped chairs on swivels arranged about a round marble-topped table. When two more guests arrive, two chairs are pulled into the circle from the dining area in the kitchen.

If you're fortunate enough to have a perfectly normal size room, arrange your seating so that it can begin with six and expand without looking cramped; in other words, leave breathing space for extra seats. This will make your room look more spacious and elegant when you're home alone and it will easily adapt to more bodies.

Suppose you like to throw cocktail parties with many more people than you have seats. Of course, most folks like to stand at cocktail parties; they can get a better view and they're more mobile—which is considered a tremendous plus factor at any big bash. I like to have what I call "occasional seats" available for perching. These are not the kind of seats you would choose for reading *War and Peace;* they are definitely for the short term. Stools, ottomans, cubes, very small chairs, all can be called upon to provide temporary sitting space.

In the living room of a client who likes to entertain, I placed one small bench, almost big enough for two narrow people, at right angles to two love seats; almost no one uses the bench except when the hostess has a big party, and then it provides instant seating. I used two movable upholstered cubes on round carpet casters which can be rolled happily with a toe between the bench and the love seats.

A friend who has very good ideas uses a spin-off of this idea. Her seating group is arranged around the fireplace, and for extra seating she has two handsome antique children's chairs. I've often perched on one of these and they are amazingly comfortable for a normal size grownup.

Dining

One of the more common problems in today's home is the lack of a proper dining room. This means that many people have their daily meals in the kitchen but must use their living room for dining with guests or special occasions.

I designed a living room where company dined at a big round Victorian table at the end of the room nearest the kitchen. The room was much longer than it was wide, and this made it possible to sequester the table in a place of its own, without dividing the space with a wall. In place of a wall, however, I used a low credenza, finished in white lacquer on both sides. It was actually an assemblage of three modular pieces. Two of these faced the dining table, holding serving things, silver, place mats, napkins and all the other paraphernalia of dining; the third section was a bar and faced the living room side. A single counter of white marble joined the three pieces and on the ceiling parallel to this counter I fastened a series of twenty small, clear cosmetic bulbs in white sockets. The bulbs were linked by a white vinyl cord which ran down the wall and plugged into a baseboard outlet. The lighting acted as a kind of sparkling divider and provided enough illumination for festive dining as well.

The point of the exercise is to let the table show; gone are the days when folks felt ashamed of allowing a dining table to show in the parlor. With the trend to multipurpose furniture and spaces, one can dine just about anywhere these days and let it all hang out. There's really nothing wrong with a dining table in the living room; in fact, it can be a big plus, because when it is not in use for its principal function it can also be used as a game table, a work table or a marvelous repository for the hundreds of magazines, books and newspapers that seem to accumulate in everyone's parlor.

Hobbies and Working

Is the living room a place you use? Could it be a room where you could be happy pursuing a hobby, working or just reading or listening to music? The reason it is important to ask and answer these questions is that it will affect the choice and location of different pieces of furniture.

If it is a room for a hobby, you will need to accommodate the hobby in a way that is consistent with the overall scheme; gone are the days when folks had to stuff their needlework or stitchery or painting or mosaic into a cupboard when the doorbell rang. In today's living room it is just as important to show that you have an interesting hobby as it is to have a beautiful room, because your hobbies are a part of your individuality and when they show, they personalize your room.

I designed a living room for a very stylish woman who was skilled at needlepoint. She had designed many commercial products in needlepoint and wanted one wall of the room to reflect her hobby. I designed a series of shelves across one whole wall and finished them in white lacquer; each space was geared to hold skeins of the yarns she used in her work. The yarns were placed in the same way that colors are arranged on the color wheel, so that the shelves melted together visually to form a great rainbow of color across the wall. This system was not only pretty, it was also practical, because it meant that the yarns could be selected easily after comparing or contrasting neighboring colors.

The shelves also held big baskets made of woven palm fronds. These baskets contained scraps of stiffened muslin, leftover yarn and colorful magazines from which this women got her design inspiration. On the upper shelves there were two speakers, covered in white linen, and a record player, as well as some baskets of the games, puzzles, crayons and paints the children liked to use. A center section of shallow, wide drawers kept finished designs flat and neat before they were transferred to the canvas; lacquered white to match the shelves, these drawers blended into the background and became part of the wall.

A work table and two comfortable chairs, one on each side of this wall unit, make it a handy place to draw and transfer designs for needlepoint, but it is also a good spot for a backgammon game or a complicated puzzle. It is a place to write a letter or pay bills or even do homework and is very comfortable for after-breakfast coffee or an afternoon cup of tea. Designed in this way, a room accommodating a specific hobby becomes a part of family life, in use day and evening, not just for needlepoint, but for the whole family.

The same principle can be applied to other uses. If you work at home, for instance, and you must have a practical place for writing or typing or seeing callers, the living room must be an office by day. This doesn't mean it has to be decked out in steel gray and plastic laminates with fluorescent lighting. A home

office can be part of your home. In fact, it can enhance your living room if you plan it properly.

I planned just such a home office for a couple where the wife had an office job and the man worked at home. He needed a desk, filing cabinets and a couple of visitors' chairs, as well as a place to type and store his many books. This turned out to be an easy assignment because the room was long and narrow and suited my purpose exactly.

I used two love seats facing one another and a pair of occasional chairs to flank the fireplace; at the far end of the room I placed a half-inch-thick glass top, the same length and height as one of the love seats directly behind it, on two white file cabinets, each of which contained one file drawer and pencil drawers. The space between them was wide enough for a comfortable swivel desk chair. A stylish typing table on casters wheels out as needed. On either side of the generous picture window behind the desk and chair I built bookshelves from the sill height to the ceiling with cupboards below to hold the many papers and supplies of a busy home office. Shelves and cupboard doors are painted white to blend with the surrounding walls and to match the file cabinets. I could have used a teakwood top for the desk and teak for the shelving and cupboard doors if the overall look of the room had required it. In this case, the couple it was designed for liked the look of chrome and glass and white backgrounds for their fine collection of African primitive sculptures and for their healthy mass of growing plants.

Even if you don't have a special hobby or a job at home, analyze how your living room can be useful to you and your family before you begin to decorate. Find a sensible place for your stereo that is off the beaten path so that you can look at record titles without having the disc snapped out of your hand by two boys and a dog racing by. Find a spot for a chair and footstool with room for a lamp and table beside it for reading a good book or the evening paper after dinner.

Find a place for your television so that it fits the seating group that you use to entertain your friends. I like my television mobile so that it serves me; I don't have to adjust myself to the set that way. I can simply move the set to a spot that is convenient for me. There are many tables that suit this purpose today—for instance, a small table on wheels that can easily handle a compact television; or if you want to be very chic, buy a cube or pedestal on casters and treat your set like a piece of valuable sculpture.

What Are the Physical Characteristics of Your Living Room?

Your lifestyle questionnaire will help you to describe and understand the physical characteristics of your living room as well as how you plan to use it.

The backgrounds for your furniture, windows, floors and walls are all important in planning a room, and we are going to go into these in greater detail in later chapters.

Windows

Windows can often pose very difficult problems for the homeowner. Take the room with windows of different sizes, a common complaint. There is a picture window on one wall and a pair of separated windows on the adjacent wall. The type of window covering you select will, of course, have a great deal to do with how much privacy or light control you require, but it is also a problem because, in addition to these functions, it must look right in your room.

I worked on a living room in a typical suburban development where the houses were a bit too close for comfort; window coverings were essential, even in the living room. For the room I designed, a very contemporary place, I chose vertical blinds, which worked perfectly at the picture window. There was a center opening, and the blinds stacked neatly on either side when a lot of light and view was needed. They completely covered the window at night.

The same window covering worked perfectly for the small windows, which I covered within the window reveal—the recess in which the window is set. If you have small windows and the reveal is not deep enough to receive a vertical blind which has three- or four-inch tapes, it's easy to build an additional one-by-four-inch frame around the window to make the whole thing look neater and built-in.

For the family with no view at all, the window covering should be able to block out the objectionable scene, be it a street or the side of another house. One system is to create what I call an "indoor view," either with a large painting or wallpaper or with a collection of small paintings and plants so interesting that the need to look outdoors is diminished. A client of mine who lived in a city apartment facing the brick wall of another building was so homesick for the New England farm he had known as a child that he painted a whole wall with the apple trees, black and white cows, barn and picket fence he remembered. He created his own view indoors.

Floors

Floors, too, are backgrounds that you must take into account. Perhaps you already have wood floors in strips or parquet. If you do, you're one step ahead, because these make marvelous settings for area rugs and furniture of any period. Treasure your wood floors; they're easy to maintain and almost indestructible. I know a misguided woman who had a house with perfect oak flooring throughout and covered every inch of it with vinyl squares patterned in mother-of-pearl. When my clients bought her house, we discovered that she had had the foresight to have the tile layed on Masonite. The floors were still intact underneath, making the instant restoration we did inexpensive.

But perhaps you don't have wood floors and you really need to cover everything with carpet. Wall-to-wall carpeting can be a glorious look, extending and stretching every inch of floor space—unless you already have the carpet and you are tired of the color. About five years ago everyone installed avocado green wall-to-wall carpet; it was like a disease that ran the length and breadth of the country, regardless of region or climate. I saw it in Anchorage and I saw it in Pensacola and it was just about the same color.

Now many of these people write to ask what they can do to change the color scheme and make it more contemporary—without junking the carpet, of course. The best way is to draw the eye away from the carpet by introducing a color scheme or pattern that is so interesting that the eye never descends as far as the carpet. Another system is to lay a smaller rug over the carpet to define the seating area. This can be a patterned rug in white, robin's-egg blue and violet, for example. Then the furniture can be re-covered to work with this, downplaying the wall-to-wall carpet by giving the focal group in the room a distinctively different color scheme, yet one that still works with the old green.

Walls

Take inventory of your walls as well. Painted dry wall is the most common variety, and it is also the easiest to change by adding one or two coats of paint.

Papered walls are more difficult. I worked on a room for a couple who called me in after they had papered the walls with a scenic wallpaper. They hated it. Fortunately, it was gray and white, and I decided to use it as a background for a crisp black and white color scheme, with a subdued hound's-tooth check on the sofa, a black, white and yellow stripe for the chairs and a large paisley print in yellow on white for the wing chair. Bright fresh yellow flowers in a white bowl on the glass-topped coffee table, a whole series of black and white prints framed in chrome with yellow mats, and clusters of potted plants and small trees in both corners of the room salvaged the room in spite of the wallpaper.

Another typical problem is the room with paneled walls. The paneling looked great in the brightly lit store, but it makes a living room facing north look like the Black Hole of Calcutta. Of course, it would be tempting to paint the paneling a bright glossy white, use a clean green, white and tangerine color scheme and create a garden room. But if you still want the wood effect, try using track lighting around the whole room to illuminate the richness of the paneling as well as to light the floor and furniture. If that's too ambitious, try four floor-based floodlights with swivels so that you can wash each wall with light from below; keep the furniture very light in color—pale beiges, off-whites and a few clear bright accents of turquoise. Your dark room will come to life again.

Personal Preferences

Art

In your lifestyle inventory you should be asking yourself about personal preferences. Taste in art, for example, is an exceedingly personal matter, and you should choose a work because you like it. That doesn't mean that you must forget your color scheme. There are purists who claim that any painting should be able to stand on its own in any color scheme, but it takes only a bit of common sense to realize that a painting that works with the colors surrounding it is going to look right in that place. If you already have the color scheme, keep it firmly in mind when looking for art; in fact, take the scheme with you in the form of small paint or fabric samples if possible. If you've fallen in love with a painting or a print, and you're ready to redecorate, try to use the work of art as a kind of springboard for your color scheme. The reason this is effective is simple: most good art is based on the same guidelines of scale, balance and color as the good design of a room.

If you already have some works of art and are not sure about where to place them, try shifting them until you come up with the right formula. I worked on a home where a large abstract painting in grays, taupes and whites had hung over a pale gray sofa for several years. After a move, the sofa was placed free standing at a right angle to the wall, and we had to find another home for the painting. It worked perfectly over the baby grand piano instead, the painting joining the piano to balance the bulk of the sofa.

Plants

Plants are so popular now that I doubt anyone would dare answer the lifestyle question in the negative; yet there are people for whom plants are too much trouble. However, as a plant lover, I feel they are worth the care they require. I've literally furnished rooms with plants; in one living room a large fiddle-leaf fig tree in a huge basket and several smaller potted plants joined a wall of books, a grand piano, two classic leather and chrome chairs and a glass and chrome coffee table to make the total furnishings. With white walls, tall windows covered with dark wood-stained shutters to match the floors and a small white flokati area rug, the room looked finished and stylish while awaiting further furniture acquisitions.

Style

Some of the most popular decorative styles are:

Art Deco	Garden	Pattern upon Pattern
Art Nouveau	Junk	Supergraphics
City	Mirror	White
Country	Natural	Wicker
Eclectic or Mix	One-Color	

Let's consider one of these, junk for example: junk is jolly, it's fun to work with and it doesn't devour your entire budget with one purchase. In fact, junk can give an ordinary room a personality and individualism no department store furniture could provide. Junk is usually classified as anything over ten years old that is not an antique (unless it happens to be an antique of no value, like a kitchen sink turned into a planter or an old wooden blueprint file converted to a coffee table). A wood and metal park bench, for example, could help bring style to a typical Lawson sofa and matching armchair. A set of four turn-of-the-century kitchen chairs around a modern white plastic table can make a splendid game center. A part of an old house, like a pediment from over a library door reduced to its natural wood finish, looks smashing as a work of art over a plain sofa.

Country means a relaxed look, with inviting seating, mellow colors and lots of patterns and real wood, either on walls or in the furniture pieces themselves. It uses bunches of flowers in crockery vases on the coffee table and accessories and finishes that work within the context—flowered or shag rugs, colored glass, wicker and stucco and painted wood finishes.

City is what country isn't. It presents an instant vision of chrome, steel and glass, marble, leather, solid colors of velvet and silk, flat-woven rugs or wall-to-wall carpeting, hard-edge large modern painting, steel sculpture, track lighting and fanciful modern lamps.

The mix is my favorite because it represents the way most of us live, liking a bit of this, a smattering of that—collected objects from all over. It is a kind of jumble of all the styles listed above, but it also has its own style. It means that you can face a pair of Barcelona chairs in tufted natural leather with a very elegant Victorian settee upholstered in a glorious rust red velour; between them is a slick chrome and white marble coffee table; and alongside the table is a marvelous bench of country French walnut, with a modern needlepoint pillow in a russet marblelike pattern. The background for this sophisticated blend (pictured on the jacket of this book) is smooth, featureless white walls and subdued lighting, but under the seating group is a fantastic Oriental Kurdish rug resplendent in its rust red background, with touches of tan and white, tying the whole color scheme together in a well-balanced island of style and chic.

Formal or Informal?

After you have thought through and decided on what to have in your living room, you must analyze your taste to determine whether you want a formal or informal arrangement. Today, there are so many different looks for living rooms that often people are tempted to try to combine them and get the most for their money. In fact, the successful rooms I have seen have all been essentially simple rooms, one look and no more.

This does not mean you have to stick rigidly to one period of furnishings—Regency or Bauhaus modern for example. The term "look," as decorators use it, means appearance or aspect. In the language of design there are two possible aspects for any room: formal or informal.

These words are often misread as neat or messy, and occasionally the two are indeed intertwined. "Formal" design implies furniture, window treatments and floor coverings which are arranged with an obvious fixed purpose and relationship. A formal room is usually set up to look just one way, and it does not adapt happily to rearrangement. There are many people I know who must have this formality in order to express themselves, though they are not necessarily formal people.

Informal design, on the other hand, means flexibility, change and variety in arrangements. In an informal room, furniture can be moved about without losing the sense of planning and organization that went into the room originally.

Remember! Formal and informal do not mean style; a very modern room can be extremely formal and a very French room can be informal. It's true, of course, that many traditional rooms are formal and fixed. But there are many modern living rooms that are equally inflexible.

The public rooms in the Governor's House at Williamsburg are a good example of traditional formality. The placement and choice of the furniture has been planned with great care to create maximum visual pleasure. These are formal rooms.

A good example of a formal contemporary room is the living room of the Tugendhat House in Brno, Czechoslovakia. Designed in 1930 by Mies van der Rohe, the great German exponent of Bauhaus architecture, this house is a milestone in the development of pure modern design. The materials—marble, ebony, beige raw silk, leather and velvet—are still earmarks of the formal modern room. The furniture, all of which is available today and still considered modern, is arranged in a group that seems permanently rooted in space, even though there is nothing at all built-in. Changing it about would be inconsistent with the design of the room.

Even built-in furniture, something we associate with informality, can give a very formal appearance to a room. A living room with a fixed seating area, no matter how contemporary the actual furniture may be, looks formal. In a room facing the sea, with a huge wall of glass in front of it, I designed a built-in sofa,

fitted into a carpeted "pit," or depression in the floor, two steps below the entry level of the house. The fixed seating, which is the only sitting furniture in the living room, is covered in gray velvet in the same shade as the carpet; it is made of white plastic laminate and is surrounded by glass and chrome tables and shining accessories. It faces the view and is angled so as to provide sociability and sitting comfort for a group of eight people. The mood is formal.

In perfect contrast to this sleek space is another room I designed for a city family. Full of mixed furniture of every conceivable period from modern to Bauhaus to Sheraton to Chippendale to Chinoiserie, it is essentially an informal room. In fact, I'm not exactly sure whether it can be labeled. I was delighted when a mutual friend took a quick look and said, "Why, it's modern!" I'll let you in on a secret: I really don't care what people call it as long as they like it.

I have talked about all this to demonstrate how important it is to know in advance what your own lifestyle demands. I hope you will find the answers to these needs in furniture arrangement, color, windows, floors, lighting and accessories in the chapters that follow.

Furniture Arrangement Comes First

Now that you have thought about your lifestyle as it relates to your living room and the furniture in it, you can start to translate these ideas into a detailed plan. Most decorators begin by actually drawing a floor plan, and this is where you should start also. Your plan must be drawn to scale from the actual measurements of the room, but don't let this artistic requirement scare you off. Floor plans are very easy to make if you follow the methods described below.

Making the Floor Plan

Tools

The most basic tool is, of course, something to measure your room with. A six-foot recoiling tape is an excellent investment for this purpose. The twelve-foot version is considerably more expensive, but it makes measuring from wall to wall much easier. I like a folding yardstick better, though, because with it you can easily measure the height of a ceiling, door or window—a job that is much more difficult with a recoiling tape. This also comes in a twelve-foot variety. Even a simple old-fashioned yardstick is a good tool for measuring walls and ceilings.

Next you will need a ruler and paper on which to make your plan. There are two basic ways to approach this part of the job. The first involves using graph paper as the basis for your scale. I recommend quarter-inch graph paper, which has four squares to the inch. With this size, you can use a scale of ¼″ = 1′ or, if you want a larger drawing, ½″ = 1′. You can buy quarter-inch graph paper in sheets which are larger than the standard 8½-by-11-inch paper. These oversized sheets are very convenient if you have a large living room because you won't have to tape or pin several sheets together.

The second approach to converting measurements involves a scale rule, which automatically converts feet into inches, half-inches or quarter-inches. This inexpensive and helpful tool enables you to use plain paper or any white drawing surface for your plan. A scale rule also makes it possible to measure inches more accurately than graph paper boxes permit, and an inch or two can make a crucial difference in a room. I once saw a plan where the headboard was just one inch too large for the wall it was designed for, making it impossible to close the bedroom door. If the measurements had been converted to inches with a scale rule instead of graph paper, this wouldn't have happened.

I have always found it useful to mount the floor plan paper on some sort of board to make it portable. Of course you can just use the kitchen table, but with a movable drawing board you can carry your floor plan around the room and work on it anywhere. A piece of Masonite is just fine for this purpose.

Don't get hung up on buying these materials at the outset. You can improvise, just as I have when I'm stuck somewhere without my drafting materials. I've made scale plans on brown paper bags, with a magazine binding or a piece of cardboard as a straightedge and a child's one-foot ruler to measure and convert the measurements. In a pinch you can even get along without a ruler. Did you know that your thumb, from the last joint to the edge of your fingernail, is approximately one inch long? Start out conservatively and work your way into professional materials after you gain a little experience.

Measuring Your Living Room

The first rule is: measure everything in inches and write the dimensions down that way. This technique lessens the chance of confusing inches and feet. If written in a hurry, "three foot six inches" looks very much like "thirty-six inches," but in a room the six-inch difference could be a major disaster. Besides, you can always convert the inches to feet and inches when you do your final plan.

In measuring a room, begin with the overall dimensions. Pick a spot where you can measure from wall to wall without running into any immovable objects. Measure the length and width of the room from molding to molding. Measure on the floor, please. Bending down can be a salutary part of decorating. You'll find there's a good bit of exercise involved in measuring a room! The reason we measure from molding to molding rather than from wall to wall is that the feet or bases of furniture often meet the molding, rather than the wall, thus cutting off that much space from the overall length or width of any room. I find it helpful to

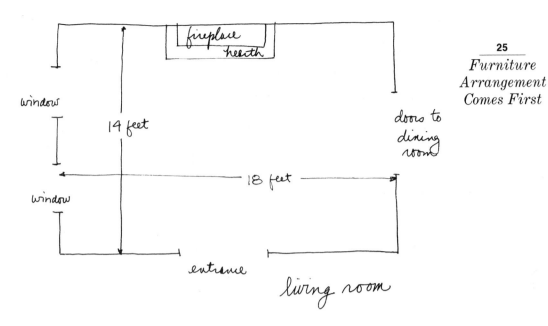

make a rough outline of the shape of the room on paper and write the dimensions, where they occur, even if they are not in scale.

After you've written down the room dimensions, begin to measure the walls. Start in one corner, and measure to the nearest opening—door, window, closet, column or alcove—and note this down on the rough plan. Continue along the wall in this way, measuring every feature, whether it is flat or at a right angle to the wall, like a column.

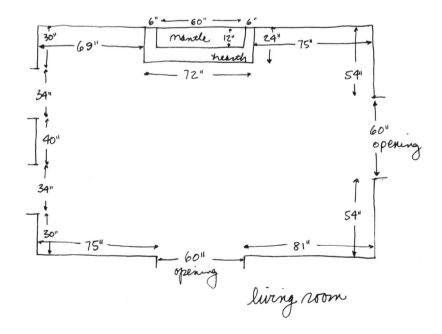

When you get to a door or a window, measure the trim or molding *with* the window or door. In other words, include the width of the trim with the width of the glass or the door. The reason for this is that designers try not to have furniture overlap trim or molding pieces. Furniture that fits against the flat part of the wall looks neater and more purposeful than if it overlaps the trim. If you are buying a new sofa, for example, it should fit cleanly on the wall, rather than overlapping a bit onto the trim of an adjoining architectural feature.

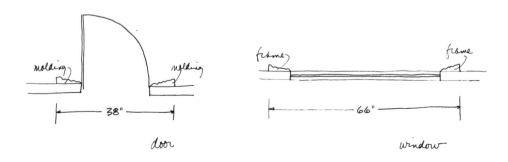

Like everything else in decorating, this is a guideline, not a rule. Don't carry it to an extreme that won't function for you. I worked on a master bedroom, for example, where there was only one wall large enough to hold the owners' two bureaus, which could not be separated either because there was no other wall at all. The wall space was a half-inch too narrow for the two bureaus to fit without overlapping the trim of the bathroom door. Did I rebuild the room? Did I rebuild the bureaus or suggest that they buy new ones? Since any other solution was impractical, I placed both bureaus on the wall, overlap and all, and just smiled.

Once you have measured the length of one wall, do the same for an adjoining wall, then the opposite wall and finally the fourth wall.

Drawing the Floor Plan

Now that you have completed the measuring, sit down at your drawing board or kitchen table and begin to draw the real plan in scale. You can use one quarter-inch or one half-inch per foot, depending on how large you want your plan to be. The average living room in half-inch scale will fit easily on one sheet of graph paper, but most people find it easier to use one quarter-inch box per foot.

It is best to convert your inch measurements into feet-and-inch combinations for the floor plan, although I've seen completely accurate and acceptable plans drawn with all-inch dimensions. When you complete the actual scale drawing of the full length of the first wall, check the total length against the overall room dimension you noted before you began to measure the individual parts of the wall. If your room is perfectly rectangular, it should match exactly, give or take an eighth of an inch or so. Do the same thing when you have drawn the first width of the room. Don't fuss over quarter-inch discrepancies. Today's builders are often careless and parallel walls may differ by as much as one inch from each other. After you have cross-checked all dimensions, you'll know you're on the right track; there's nothing worse than drawing a room and finding that the two parallel walls turn out to be different dimensions. If that happens, you have made a mistake somewhere in your measuring.

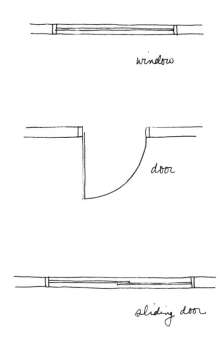

window

door

sliding door

To finish the drawing of any room, you must indicate the architectural features with special symbols. A window is drawn with two parallel lines close together. A door is drawn ajar, indicating where it hinges and which way it opens. A sliding door is indicated by two parallel lines close together, like a window, but they overlap at the center a bit.

Planning Your Furniture Arrangement

With your newly made floor plan, accurate and to scale, you can plan your furniture arrangement. After years of working with students and using classroom techniques, I have learned that the easiest way is to cut furniture shapes out of thin cardboard and move them around within the floor plan until you find an arrangement you like. Use colored cardboard which is different enough from the white paper of your plan to show the outlines of the pieces.

To make the furniture, measure each piece you own and want to use in your room exactly as you have measured the walls—the length and width in inches. Using your scale rule, convert these into quarter-inch or half-inch scale outlines on cardboard, then label and cut out each cardboard piece.

Now you will have to make shapes for the furniture you don't have but will be acquiring in the future. This is easy if you have made up your mind and know exactly what piece you want—just go and measure it in the store. If you know what *kind* of piece but haven't picked out the specific one, just measure a typical example in the store. Furniture sizes like sofa lengths and table widths are pretty standard, so you can't go too far wrong in doing this. If you have only the vaguest notion about the piece, estimate the size according to what you think you will need or want—or what fits best in your plan.

Once you have all your furniture drawn and cut out, begin your layout. In arranging furniture, keep in mind that there are three basic criteria: *scale,* or the relationship of the size of a piece of furniture to its space and to other furniture; *function,* or how people will use the furniture for conversation, work or pleasure; and *traffic patterns,* or the paths in the room between the furniture for people to pass through.

This may sound very mechanical and not at all esthetic, but I have found that the tools and techniques of design, though quite pedestrian and certainly unexciting, can be combined to produce beautiful, artistic rooms.

Scale

A few guidelines about scale are all you really need to make a value judgment about the size of furniture you are buying or that you already have. Scale is a puzzling concept because it cannot be estimated except by those who have years of experience, and even then they can goof. You see, the size of a piece of furniture can look amazingly different in different surroundings. I have a big bedroom, and my parents have one that is considerably smaller. For years my mother has been trying to unload a chaise longue that was too long and wide for her room. When I moved, she asked me if I'd like the chaise and I eagerly accepted, since my room was relatively unfurnished. When she saw the chaise in my room she said, ''But it looks so small!'' And it does, simply because it is more in scale with the dimensions of the new room.

The mechanical aspect of scale can be measured by including in your floor plan the length and width of every piece of furniture you plan to use in your room. This is essentially a job for the drawing board—measuring and drawing and seeing how the dimensions of each piece fit with the other pieces and with the overall dimensions of the room. Practicing with cut-out cardboard furniture within the outline drawing of your room will help you get a feeling of the mechanical side of scale.

Of course, scale has a third dimension, which is height. Height is more important than you realize. In the average room of today, most furniture is approximately thirty inches above the floor. This is the height that supports our backs when we are seated and the height we use for most of our work or dining tables. Of course, there are lower seats and tables, but they are well below our standing eye level. One of the reasons why your room may appear unexciting and uninteresting is that the furniture is all roughly the same height. Check your living room. Wouldn't it be more interesting if you had a series of high and low points in the room? The stimulus of changing heights is as meaningful to the eye as a bright color or an unusual pattern. This is the esthetic aspect of scale.

It isn't easy to find high furniture these days, because most pieces are designed for our small living rooms. There are a few ways to beat the height problem, however. A tall secretary-desk is a beautiful accent in an otherwise low room; a baby grand piano is another, particularly if you leave it open, with the top elegantly thrust up. A storage wall for books and stereo from ceiling to floor can work. A tall tree gives imposing height to an area, and a cluster of hanging baskets can do the same thing.

One of my favorite devices is to use a large bureau as a storage unit in a living room. A four-drawer dresser of unusual design can be a marvelous addition to a parlor when placed near a contemporary sofa and chairs, especially if it looks even faintly antique. I've found a lot of these biggies in secondhand stores. These pieces are also practical because they can hold supplies for the living room, games, papers, magazines, puzzles and junk.

Lamps can also bring height to a room. This doesn't mean you should buy those thirty-six- or forty-inch-high monster table lamps. Instead of a tall fat lamp on a table, why not a tall thin lamp on the floor? Better proportioned and less obtrusive, a tall floor lamp can illuminate as easily as a big lamp and still provide the necessary height.

A hanging lantern, one of my favorites, is a good way to take the eye up. Buy an inexpensive Japanese white paper lantern, about eighteen inches in diameter. You can wire this yourself with the proper length of electric cord, a cord switch and a plug at the end. The socket and cord are easy to assemble

and you can hang this relatively weightless combination from the ceiling, on a sturdy cup hook, wherever you need the light. Then loop the cord to the wall with the nearest baseboard outlet.

A lighting fixture over a table in a corner can also add height to a room, but don't get carried away. Use hanging lamps sparingly and always in a corner or over a table where people will be sitting. There is nothing more distracting than having a great huge lantern dangling over a coffee table where people who are likely to be standing about must try to dodge the silly thing while they attempt to make sensible conversation.

Anything applied directly to the wall above furniture adds to its height. A large picture, a collection of smaller, framed pictures or of objects that interest you, a sculpture on a tall pedestal—all these add height to space. Of course, this third dimension of scale is hard to imagine without some help. But with your new know-how, you can eliminate the guesswork by drawing what designers and architects call "elevations" of any wall in your living room.

To do this, you measure the wall exactly as you did the floor, except you must also measure the height of the ceiling and the doors, windows or other openings, as well as the furniture you plan to use. If you have already measured the length of the wall in question for your floor plan, draw this length as a straight line on your paper. Now measure the height of the wall.

Measure the heights of windows and doors next and, assuming you already have their widths, you can draw these elements in scale on your plan, which is actually what an elevation is—a vertical plan.

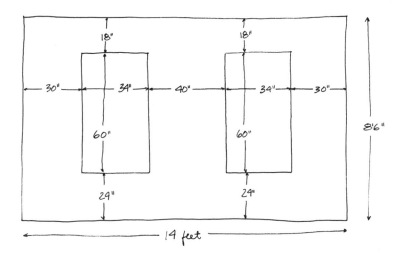

Suppose you decide that you want to surround a low sofa with elements that give height to the space. Draw the length and height of the sofa as a rectangle on your elevation. On one side draw the table which is next to the sofa. Disregard the table's contours—all you need to record for the moment is the height and width or length of the piece. On the other side of the sofa draw a rough outline of the tall floor lamp you plan to buy—certainly you measured its height when you were considering it at the store? Now consider your elevation. Does the lamp look too tall? Too short? Perhaps it looks absurd towering in lonely splendor on one side of the sofa. Try a good-sized picture over the sofa—either one you have that goes with the color of the room or one you have seen—and draw its outline in proper scale over the sofa. Still look silly? Try a tall tree at the other end of the sofa, with a couple of smaller plants clustered at the base, to balance the scale of the lamp. Hopefully, the tree will be near a window so it will thrive as well as improve the outlook.

Have you always wanted a storage wall but you never knew quite how to plan it? An elevation is the ideal way to begin. Choose a wall that is preferably without openings like doors and windows, and draw it in scale. Then take time out to make a list of what must go on it and measure *all* the dimensions of these items. Depth is often a crucial dimension, so it is important to have a floor plan view of the items on the wall as well.

I worked on a storage wall for a living room where the owner wanted a complicated tape system, storage for five hundred tapes, the necessary receiver and speakers, a drop-down writing surface and a drop-down bar surface, shelves for books and a color television. On the elevation everything fitted nicely, but when I developed a floor plan for this elevation, the depth required for the color television was much too great for the room, as well as for the other parts to be housed in the unit. We compromised and subtracted the television, placing it on a mobile cube, which turned out to be more convenient anyway.

In another living room that I designed for a couple with two young children, I was appalled when I saw the number of spare parts scattered about the room—a record player on a small table, two speakers on the floor nearby, a television on a bench, records in stacking boxes on another wall, a tiny desk left over from another era and games just piled on the floor. It was obviously time for a storage wall! With a bit of help, the owners made an elevation of a perfect blank wall, measured their many scattered parts and discovered that an inexpensive modular system available at a local furniture store would fit their needs and their space like a glove. They installed the unit themselves and saved lots of money and time by developing their needs according to a plan.

With this kind of scaling in plans and elevations, you can easily decide in advance what to buy or what to move in a room, whether on the floor or on the wall. You have made a three-dimensional picture of your living room, and you will be referring to this frequently as you become more and more experienced in designing your own home.

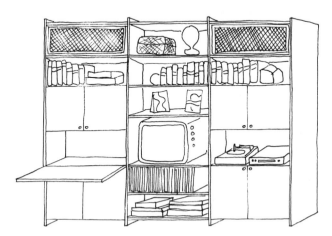

Function

Planning the furniture arrangement in your room involves *function.* Remember that pieces of furniture function in three ways: as anchors, as dividers and as communicators. Anchors always come first. Every room needs at least one—a piece of furniture that establishes place or stability for a grouping because of its scale. The other pieces of the grouping can be smaller and lighter and obviously mobile.

A sofa is a good example of an anchor, whereas the table in front of it or beside it and the chairs arranged about it are definitely "floatable." A piano is an anchor, and the pair of occasional chairs nestling in its curve are floaters. Just try to imagine for a moment what a room would look like without anchors! I conjure up a vision of those grand ballrooms at Versailles with many elegant little chairs lining the walls. It reminds me of a living room I once saw where all the furniture was small and seemed to float high above the floor, including a flyweight sofa.

Placing an anchor on your plan means looking for undisturbed areas where this large piece can do its thing. First look for a good wall, large enough for the sofa and its companion floaters. If there is no wall handy to receive your sofa-anchor, you can *create* a wall by floating the sofa somewhere in the central space of the room. Remember that a free-standing sofa is as much an anchor as one that is wall-based, because its back takes the place of the wall your room lacks.

How does furniture work as a divider? The word "divider" has come to mean any shelf system that separates one part of a room from another. But almost anything can become a divider, even your sofa. Take the hypothetical room with no wall large enough to back up your sofa. You've placed it free of walls, and in this way you can use the space behind it for something else, like the game table for Monopoly, or a music corner with a reclining chair where you and your stereo can reside undisturbed, or a plant corner or hobby center. In other words, if you can leave enough space behind it and you need this space for a function other than just plain seating, your anchoring sofa has itself become a divider.

You can convert other pieces into dividers as well. A low storage unit that acts as a bar on one side can be a "wall" on the other, providing a separate space for dining in the living room without interrupting the flow of space. A cluster of low plants, a decorative soup tureen and a clump of handsome candlesticks on the top of the unit can, make it work on all sides, like a piece of free-standing sculpture. Of course, not all storage pieces are finished on their back sides, but that shouldn't stop you. You can carpet the back with leftovers from your floor, using spray cement or double-faced tape. Or you can paper the back, or tile it with decorative Spanish tiles, or simply finish it like the rest of the piece by adding a flush plywood section and staining or painting it to match.

Pieces of furniture act as communicators by their relationships. When you are planning your conversation group, for example, it would scarcely do to have every piece plastered against a wall. Furniture must be planned to relate in order to communicate. If you have a sofa with two low armchairs on one side at a right angle to it, place another pair of occasional chairs opposite these on the other side of the sofa. Then you have a classic situation for perfect communication—the U-shape—and you can seat seven or eight without dragging in extra chairs from the dining room.

In some rooms, an L-shaped group is all there is space for. Make it inviting by using soft, modular seating flanked protectively around an ample coffee table. You might even have a spare foot or two for a mobile ottoman—not exactly the epitome of comfort but it adds an extra seat.

Storage walls can be communicators by their instant announcement of function. They may contain lots of books, thus communicating that this is a living room where reading is taken seriously, or they may be stereo centers, accommodating the many parts necessary to communicate sound. Storage walls can provide displays, with shelves creating separate alcoves for the goodies you have collected on your travels and closed storage below providing room for the pieces you will display six months from now. Or this kind of

wall may simply communicate that this is a busy, happy family because it includes a place to work, a serving center, a niche for the family television and plenty of shelf space for books, plants, games and objets d'art.

Traffic

The final consideration in your furniture arrangement is what I call "indoor traffic." Every room, no matter how small, has a traffic path that must be kept free and clear. There is nothing more frustrating than tripping over a chair leg while running to answer the phone or catch the milkman. Traffic patterns are very logical; there is no trick in deciding how to get from one space to another. This doesn't mean that all your furniture should be pasted cautiously against the walls so that an entire battalion can thunder through. Most traffic, in fact, is single. It's very rare that two or more people will promenade through a living room at the same time, so you needn't allow a six-lane highway between chair and sofa. I like to leave about three feet clear for the traffic path. You'll find that this will not take much space from your living room and you can almost always plan around it. Of course, there are rooms where getting from one part to another presents a very definite problem, and these call for drastic rethinking of the furniture plan.

In one room I worked on, the living room was divided exactly in half at the entry door by a careless builder. On one side there was a pleasant window and on the other side a matching window and a corner fireplace. It was obvious that a central furniture group was out of the question because the path to the dining area and the kitchen behind it would have to be forged right through the middle of the room.

I used two groups instead of one—a small one parallel to the face of the fireplace containing a love seat and two chairs, and at the other end, a sofa and three chairs. Actually, although entertaining for a group of six or eight people means moving chairs, it makes a great party room because the traffic path is

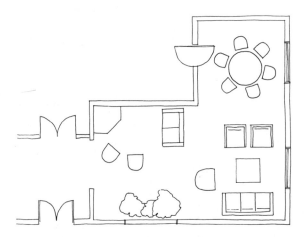

clearly indicated. The entire party can break up into two happy groups and have easy access to food and drink in the dining room.

Traffic also has to do with the distance between pieces of furniture or the space between furniture and nearby walls. A coffee table, for example, should not be further than about eighteen inches from the sofa or chairs it serves. This space should leave ample room to maneuver between the two pieces yet not be too wide for a person to reach comfortably for a glass or an ashtray.

Similarly, don't squish a dining table and chairs into too little space. Allow thirty to thirty-six inches behind the back of a chair to get in and out. If the space is really small, cut down on the table size; a larger table would look out of scale with the space anyway. These clearance measurements are indicators of scale that act as warning signals as you draw your furniture plan. If it looks crowded, begin to measure clearances carefully.

Working with Your Floor Plan

You have your plan in front of you. Out of cardboard cut a sofa that fits the room. Seven feet long by three feet wide is a good beginning, though you may need one that is longer or shorter depending on the dimension of the longest wall. Place the sofa where it can become the focus of a functioning conversation group. Remember that a sofa is essentially a social piece of furniture; although it is admittedly a wonderful place to stretch out full length, its more acceptable use is for two or more people to sit together and socialize. Place a pair of comfortable chairs opposite the sofa, separated from it by a coffee table, with two occasional chairs on either side of the sofa to form a group, or conversation area. These can be drawn to scale, labeled and cut from your cardboard.

Perhaps your room is too narrow for this square arrangement, which takes up at least eleven feet of width in the room. Or perhaps you need a passage to get by the conversation group. Try cutting out two love seats, approximately five feet long and three feet wide, and placing them opposite one another at right angles to the long wall. Arrange two occasional chairs, about two feet by two feet, to form a generous U-shaped group around a coffee table. This group occupies only about eight or nine feet in width. Don't stretch the pieces in the group too far apart. Remember that one of the most important parts of socializing is conversation, and if you are more than eight or nine feet apart you cannot converse without raising your voice. A good rule is that the back-to-back distance between facing pieces of furniture in a conversation group should not be more than twelve feet. You can measure this distance on the floor plan with your scale rule, then place the two love seats in the most pleasant relationship.

Don't be afraid of the two-love-seat substitute for a conventional sofa. More and more people are using this system, or the equally flexible substitute of one love seat and two matching armchairs. This combination provides more

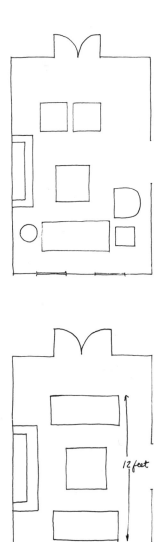

flexibility in furniture arrangement, particularly if you, like most Americans, are constantly on the move and can't tell what shape your next living room will have.

If the two love seats look lonely on the long wall, fill in the corners behind each with additional seating—a round table and two small armchairs, for example, or a game table and four chairs if you have room. Perhaps you can use one of these empty corners for a piano or a desk and storage combination. If you work at home, this may be the perfect solution. In one living room I designed, I used the twin-love-seat system rather than a sofa because the room was very long and very narrow. Between the love seats was a square glass-topped coffee table which gave plenty of surface without looking bulky. Two small French armchairs joined the love seats, and on the fourth side, I used three square ottomans on casters for extra seats or for tired feet at the end of a long day. Behind one of the love seats I placed a glass-topped desk and type-writer stand because this living room belonged to two young people who both worked, and the wife wrote freelance stories at home. Behind the other love seat I built a platform of plywood on one-by-six boards and carpeted it with the same carpet as the rest of the room. This five-foot-square platform contains a beautiful cello and music stand, since the husband is a serious musician and enjoys chamber music. There is even room on this platform for a neighbor—a violinist who comes over periodically for evening sessions.

Empty corners can also be filled with plants, high and low, or sculpture on a pedestal. Corners are marvelous places for secondary accent pieces, or a purely frivolous grouping of things, that act as a frame for the primary accent—the sofas and chairs that form the conversation grouping.

All these pieces will fall into place when you combine your new working tools—the lifestyle analysis and the floor plans and elevations. You will surely be successful with this system because it is the very same one used by professional designers.

Plan Ahead

Once you have analyzed your lifestyle and made your floor plan, begin to plan—and I mean plan ahead. Just as Rome wasn't built in a day, do not expect to finish your living room in one big sweep.

Although one out of five Americans moves every year, most of us do stay put for longer than that, and five years is a sensible period to plan for. It is long enough to stretch your furnishing budget, but short enough to realize your goal. Don't worry, it sounds longer than it really is!

Some people don't understand how the five-year plan works. They think it means that the room will be unfinished until the five years are almost up. On the contrary, a cleverly arranged five-year plan will provide a living room that looks complete to everyone who sees it—only you will know that there are gaps to fill.

Planning a Five-Year Program

The first step in developing a budget for this long-term plan is to make a list. Decide first what you are keeping: Do the pieces need refinishing or reupholstery? Then ask yourself how much of your yearly income you will be able to allocate to furnishing your living room.

Now you can begin to price the things you plan to buy. Keep in mind that even though politicians promise to hold back the tide of inflation, prices will probably go up roughly 8 to 10 percent each year. Add another 10 percent for contingencies. That is the catchall category for mistakes, changing your mind and buying the higher-priced fabric for the chair or adding a lamp or an expensive ashtray.

Having decided what to keep and what to buy, make a chart like this one:

Five-Year Plan

Function

Seating	Furniture on Hand	Furniture Needed	Budgeted Out	Buy Now	Buy Later
1					
2					
3					
4					
5					
Surfaces					
1					
2					
3					
4					
Storage					
1					
2					
3					
Window Covering					
Floor Covering					
Wall Covering					

This chart doesn't even cover accessories like decorative pillows, bowls, boxes, baskets or all the little things that make a living room look like you. I am assuming that you have already collected or will be collecting these as you go along.

The most important thing to remember as you work on your chart is that you should invest first in the things that count most, like sofas or lounge chairs. These are the anchors of your room; the other pieces can be improvised or temporary. You can create a perfectly beautiful coffee table for very little money by buying a thirty-six-inch round glass top for an eighteen-inch cube you make yourself out of painted plywood. Or you can improvise an attractive desk from painted plywood, with a top wrapped in felt supported by two wooden sawhorses.

Of course, planning ahead requires thinking ahead. In addition to your chart of what to buy now and later, you must think ahead about color. If you keep the major furniture pieces in neutrals you will have the greatest flexibility. This may sound very "blah," but think over the possibilities for a moment. Neutral includes the range of colors from black, brown, gray, taupe, charcoal, tan and beige to off-white and white. The textures can range from rough white wool to thick pearl gray velour to brown linen, from taupe and white herringbone tweed to charcoal homespun, from tan canvas to beige or off-white moiré, silk or polished cotton. Leathers and fake leathers in natural colors make marvelously flexible coverings which can be placed anywhere in your home.

The fact that you've clothed your furniture in this subtle range of colors does not mean the room must be colorless. In a library–living room I worked on, the furniture is covered in chocolate brown velour and the rug is a tan and white pattern. Two chairs are covered in natural leather that looks a lot like the rug color, and at the windows I used burnt bamboo roll-up blinds. The room has high ceilings and not much character so I painted it Greek red. This is the color that the Parthenon was when it was first built twenty-five hundred years ago—a kind of rust red that is very cozy and makes the room just right for good music, lots of talking and a glass or two of white wine. Some of the things in the room are temporary. For example, I used as a coffee table a lacquer table that is too small for the room and too high for the sofas but that will be used as a bedside table later on when the owners can spend the money for the very expensive, low glass Italian coffee table I have my eye on right now. This purchase may be deferred for a year or more because the temporary arrangement looks just fine.

One of the most important things to remember is that no matter how few pieces you buy the first or second year, the room must look complete and beautiful at every stage of its development. Planning ahead involves more than a single floor plan; it means that you must make a floor plan for each year of your five-year plan. This is your ultimate goal and your chart is going to organize the steps you must take to reach it. Now you must make it work visually. Let's work out a typical five-year plan as an example.

The First Year

Begin with the furniture you have or will be buying the first year and arrange these pieces in the best way you can to make the room work for you. If you're short of furniture, which most people are the first year, float it. This means that rather than placing the sofa, the most significant piece you have bought, against a wall where it looks small, place it at a right angle to a wall. Let it stand free of the walls and become the anchor for the two occasional chairs you already own which might be re-covered in the same fabric as the new sofa, or might be a pair of director's chairs from the dining room. Not only does the sofa look very much larger floating in space, it also gives you the option of backing it up later on with the narrow console you now own, which is doing its thing against the wall, holding stereo receiver and record player and acting as a part-time bar. Or you could fill the space beyond the sofa with a tall tree and low, bushy plants in a thick cluster.

Maybe the wall looks blank with the sofa at a right angle to it, particularly if you don't have a fireplace to use as a focus for this free-standing group. Make a focal point of your own—hang a handsome area rug or if you really want to economize, frame a few yards of a large-patterned fabric by wrapping it around a big canvas stretcher such as painters use.

If your room is large and you still think the furniture looks skimpy, use a tried and true decorating trick. Paint the whole room in a deep tone, like brown or navy blue. This tends to foreshorten the space by bringing the walls closer visually. Paint can often take the place of furniture. It is the greatest and least expensive space filler, and when you finally acquire the pieces you want you can repaint the walls white or cover them with wallpaper, paneling or even fabric.

Instead of costly window treatments, you might use simple shades at your windows. Treat the window in an unusual way by framing in the entire window from ceiling to floor to add height to the room and then carrying the shade from ceiling to floor as well. This is the kind of do-it-yourself project that even I can handle. For the frame, all you need is 1¼-by-6-inch stock lumber, precut to the size you need by your local lumberyard, and a handful of long nails to go with your hammer. The frame is applied with the thin edge perpendicular to the wall, to give depth to the window. In the third or fourth year, when you feel you have the extra money, you can always buy draperies or experiment with something like shutters or cloth-covered hinged panels on either side of the window. The point is that the simple frame and shade treatment costs very little but will give the room a finished look for as long as it is necessary.

Another idea is to buy a set of dining chairs and use the two armchairs as a pair of occasional chairs in the living room. An even less expensive idea is to use a pair of director's chairs in natural wood with white canvas seats and backs. These can go on a terrace in the summer or fold away for extra seating as your five-year plan advances.

Remember that chairs, like all pieces of furniture, are your slaves, to be moved or used at your will. Don't ever feel obligated to a piece of furniture—just because you bought it for your dining room or your deck doesn't mean you can't use it in your parlor.

The Second Year

The second year brings its scheduled changes. The narrow console you used against one of the blank walls, which has been acting as a hi-fi station plus bar, is now shifted to its new place behind the sofa. In its stead you construct a storage wall. This marvelous arrangement, which fills the wall from corner to corner, is every homeowner's blissful dream. It not only incorporates the stereo parts that were formerly perched precariously on the narrow console, but it also houses the speakers at proper spacing, provides a drop-down bar where a great many party things can be stored as well and has an alcove deep enough to receive a good-sized television. Best of all, it is a place to catalog and display the many books that have been shut away in cartons for a year, as well as the many attractive objets d'art you may have collected and continue to garner on your travels. At one end of the storage wall another drop-down section provides ample writing and storage space for letters and bills; a clamp-on lamp makes the space workable. All in all, it is a working wall, and it was scheduled for the second year of the five-year plan because it was difficult to imagine living without it.

There are many different kinds of storage walls, from the most expensive custom variety made by a cabinetmaker, which cost about a hundred dollars minimum per linear foot, to the many ready-made storage wall components at much lower prices, which work admirably in most situations. There is also the kind you can make yourself with standards, brackets, shelving and unfinished cupboards. No matter which you decide on, keep in mind three considerations. The first is that the units fit your needs. This means that you must list and measure all the things you plan to house in your new wall. The second is practicality; surfaces that are used for work or a bar should be plastic-laminated. This is not difficult since most speciality and department stores sell prelaminated shelves. The third consideration is whether to buy a wall-mounted system or the self-supporting type, and this depends on how your walls are constructed. If you're in doubt, ask a knowledgeable friend or the builder.

The storage wall you chose is very pale white oak and comes in stock modules. This makes a smashing contrast with the other three walls and yet will look just fine when the room is later converted to a combination of white stuccolike finish and oak paneling, the plan for the fourth year.

The Third Year

During the third year, take a critical look at backgrounds. Up comes the red shag carpet that came with the apartment. It is still perfectly good, particularly the sections that weren't part of the traffic pattern, and will be a happy addition to the master bedroom, which desperately needs wall-to-wall carpeting to make it look larger. For the living room, however, we are going to refinish the floors (originally a kind of yellowed parquet) with a deep English oak brown stain. This is a relatively costly project that will make an enormous visual difference to the room, enriching everything within sight. Yet the resulting surface is very easy to maintain with occasional buffing and a rare waxing job.

Mirrored paneled screens, a double-hinged pair for each window, flank the windows just outside the narrow frames made in the first year. These do many things for the living room. They add height by being strongly vertical elements; their mirrored finish adds sparkle and depth to the room; and they take the place of draperies which are a bother to maintain and just about as expensive as the panels. And the panels are reversible. The other side is painted a bright light green so that in summer they can be reversed and turn the room into a summer bower without adding a slipcover or a new pillow. The white window shades remain, to keep out too much sun in summer and to give privacy, but in front of them we hang bamboo blinds in a natural finish that looks marvelous with the white walls and dark floors.

The Fourth Year

In the fourth year you invest in some good furniture, the kind that is so classic it can go with anything at all. I like the wraparound leather chairs of Le Corbusier, the great French architect who was one of the pioneers of modern design, because their style and soft glovelike leather work with any kind of furniture style. You splurged and bought an elegant game table and the pair of brass reading lamps that flank the sofa. The furniture is rearranged so that the sofa faces the accent wall and is flanked by the new armchairs on one side and the game table and its pair of occasional chairs on the other. At the end of the fourth year, you invested in a smashing large painting that makes it possible to take down the framed fabric that had substituted for it for so long. Actually, this fabric was cut up into the covering for a huge floor pillow that makes an extra seat for the limber few who come to cocktail parties.

The Fifth Year

In the fifth year, you splurge again and buy a fantastic Oriental rug to make a glorious pool of color, pattern and just plain splendor for the seating group, which has again been shifted about. The sofa faces the storage wall and is backed up by the console that doubled as a hi-fi and bar combination in the first year. The wall behind the sofa is paneled in flat-cut oak in its natural finish, to match the storage wall, and the other two walls have been painted white, with a bit of sand added to the paint to give it a textured stuccolike appearance. For the final addition, you lost your head and bought two fabulous real antiques, a pair of French fauteuils (small open-arm chairs), and these are covered in an elegant pearl gray suede. One of the old occasional chairs is used as a desk chair, the other went to the bedroom.

A track light has been added to the ceiling at each end of the room. At one end it accents the richness of the oak storage wall, and makes it possible to read the titles of the books or see how you're making the perfect martini. The track on the opposite wall enriches the oak paneling and will, in the future, illuminate a fine collection of black and white drawings that you have just begun to collect now that the five-year plan is completed.

Color Comes Second

Even if you are armed to the teeth with books and magazines, or have just become an accomplished draftsman, none of these count if you ignore the all-important aspect of color.

Once you have mastered the simple concepts of space planning, you must tackle the much more complicated concept of color planning. The reason that color planning is complex is that, unlike space planning, there are few objective rules or guidelines for color decisions; the choice of color is individual and subjective. Each of us has a very different and unique set of visual responses to color, since our very eyes react individually to it. In fact, let's face it, there is absolutely no way of knowing whether the color I call red is the color you call red.

My own feelings about color are personal and intense and I am going to share them with you in this chapter. I am not going to explain color theory in the classical terms you occasionally hear, like "value," "chroma" or "hue." I shall not discuss color schemes in terms like "analogous" or "double-complementary." Instead, I am going to use plain language in talking about color so we can explore how you react to it and how to use it for the best result.

How You React to Color

All of us need to know more about color because it affects our visual environment more than any other single quality. Color is used as a signal because it speaks in a universal language that everyone understands. Consider the traffic light, the exit sign, the flashing yellow blinker. When we see these signals, we react to color in our environment. Similarly, we react with pleasure to the red-orange-pink glow of a sunset, or the special brilliance of a green lawn when the sun is just beginning to set, or the fantastic intensity of a bunch of anemones in a vase on a table, or the incredible radiance of a New England autumn. What does this response mean in the design of our homes? Surveys made for major manufacturers of many different kinds of products indicate clearly that color is the major reason why people prefer one type of product over another. This is especially true in both home and body fashion. About twenty years ago, price was the single major factor in preference, but today price is second to color.

Other buying habits are often greatly influenced by color; cars are a good example. We are all very careful to inform ourselves about the price, mileage and performance characteristics of a car we are about to buy, but aren't we also just a bit influenced by its color? Cleaning products, vacuum cleaners, dishwashers, refrigerators—all of these are products that appear in a galaxy of colors that have been thoroughly researched before they make their final appearance in the store. The proposed color of containers for new products is the subject of an entire research and development program conducted full-time. In fact, you would be amazed at how often you are being tested for color preference in products without even knowing it. Take carpeting, for example. The mill may produce a line of carpet in twenty-two colors, but after a year of preferential testing on the market the number of colors may be reduced to eighteen, or several new ones may be substituted before the line is really established.

The main reason why color is considered so important in the manufacture of products for the home is that the consumer has an instant emotional response to color. In fact, we react more *emotionally* to it than to any other characteristic. It is common to hear someone comment that she loves or hates red or blue or yellow or green. This intensity of feeling rarely develops for a texture or a style or a pattern. I don't believe I've ever heard anyone express hatred for a plush textured carpet or a velvet fabric or a Queen Anne chair leg or a paisley pattern.

Of course, we all have preferences in style, or in texture, or in pattern. But the language used in expressing these preferences pales alongside the words we used to describe color. Expressions like the following are not uncommon: olive green is disgusting; orange is incredibly vulgar; I wouldn't have pink in my room if you paid me a million dollars; bright green makes me feel sick; I can't stand gray; brown depresses me.

Most of us are quite sure of our preferences, violent or otherwise. What we don't realize, of course, is that any color is beautiful when it is used correctly. The person who hates olive green might feel considerably less disgusted if it was used in a pleasing way. Picture a room with robin's-egg blue walls and lots of white woodwork; fabric patterns with olive green, similar blues and perhaps violet purple against a white ground; bleached French country furniture; and an olive green carpet to bring the whole thing together. This lovely combination might bring about a completely new reaction to the use of olive green.

The person who thinks orange is vulgar might actually enjoy it as an accent in pillows, bowls, flowers or a painting in an otherwise neutral modern room with off-white canvas upholstery, a mirrored coffee table and a cowhide rug on polished wood floors.

Pink, a color usually associated with a sexist view of baby girls, can be incredibly beautiful as a tint. Put just a touch of red in a pot full of otherwise white paint and use it for woodwork and ceiling. Walls tinted pink can be an elegant background for browns, deep winey reds and colors more closely related like salmon, peach or rose, and pink serves as a good background for art.

Anyone who feels sick at the sight of bright green has never seen it in action in a room with white walls, white ceiling and a white shag rug; or in a room full of airy wicker furniture which has a bright green and white trellis pattern on the upholstery; or in masses of ferns growing in baskets, brilliant white ceramic pots or sparkling crystal or glass containers.

Gray is a very undervalued color. It is the most subtle and most difficult to work with because it is an understated color. Yet a room painted gray, with a matching velvety carpet, makes an instant statement of elegance. It also makes a perfect background for several different styles of furniture—a gray background would be as perfect for contemporary things as it would for a room full of fine French antiques. Why? The neutrality of gray acts very much like a mirror; it is a blank until an object is set before it, and then it magnifies and glorifies by reflecting the essential style of the object without offering any color impact. In this way, steel and glass or felt and marble will adapt perfectly to gray, as will an elegant fruitwood fauteuil with a needlepoint seat and back, an olivewood chest with ormolu hardware or a pale pastel painting in the Impressionist style.

Brown is a neutral as well, but it makes more demands on its furnishings. First of all it is dark, and used on walls it has an immediate emotional impact. For the person who feels depressed by dark walls but wants to try this high-fashion color, I would prescribe a rich chocolate-sauce brown with white woodwork and a white ceiling. The floor can be oak strips, painted with a good quality white paint and then covered with a few coats of polyurethane sealer. When I first heard about this process from a friend who has impeccable taste I asked with some cynicism how her white floors were wearing. "Perfectly," she smiled. "What about the children and the dogs?" I asked. "No problem," she answered, "they use the floor like a gym, and if the weather is bad and mud is tracked in, I just mop it up." But even if you're not brave enough for white wood floors, you could stain them dark and use a generous area rug of woven off-white Irish hemp. Or install a white vinyl floor and then use modern or traditional furniture in neutral, pale off-whites or matching dark brown with touches of coral or lavender or cerulean blue as accents.

There are, indeed, colors that are difficult to use in a living room. Take true, bright red, for example, or royal blue or emerald green. These are colors that have a high intensity, and it would be hard to work them into a color scheme as a dominant factor. A good common-sense approach to color would indicate that there are colors to be used sparingly, as accents. True red is an impossible color for a living room wall, carpet or sofa, but a large modern abstract painting in this color would be a marvelous focal point in an otherwise neutral room. Royal blue and emerald green make sensational accents; two bowls on a coffee table, a needlepoint pillow with the blue as a background for a white design and a lacquered box on an occasional table are about all the bright blue or green you need in a color scheme that is basically pale pastels or even white.

Keep an open mind on color. I like to think about the child who said she liked pink and red and mauve and purple best, but next year she hoped to like green best, too.

How to Use Color in Your Room

If you're ready for a fresh color scheme, explore new ideas. Discard all your old prejudices and look at each color as a part of an entire plan.

Three Basic Schemes

There are three major color paths that you may choose from—dark, light and bright. These are elementary and easy to imagine. A dark scheme is one that makes use of deep, rich color; for example, combine rust walls with a dark bottle green accent, a bit of burnt orange velvet upholstery on a Victorian settee and a deep amber highlight from a glass lampshade. In contrast, a light scheme might include ivory walls with a caramel leather sofa, a travertine marble coffee table, an old bleached oak secretary, antelope-colored wall-to-wall carpeting and accents of lemon yellow or peachy pink. The bright path uses a strong color as a dominant part of the theme. White walls, for instance, are a crisp background for a brilliant paisley pattern in vermilions, yellow and white on the sofa. Perhaps this scheme includes smaller patterns in similar colors on smaller pieces of furniture, an enormous modern painting with bright yellow as the principal color and a huge bunch of yellow marigolds in a white vase on a glass-topped table.

From these basic paths you can derive many subtle spin-offs. The too-dark room can be brightened by tiny accents of more intense color or lightened by painting woodwork white. A bright room that lacks impact can be shaded by staining the floorboards deep walnut brown and introducing dark brown as a small accent—in wood sculpture or carved boxes or a large basket stained dark brown to hold a tree. The overly bright room can be diminished by tinting the white walls with a tiny dollop of red or yellow to lessen the contrast of walls and

upholstery, or by exchanging the vermilion for a softer shade of orange red or a paler yellow.

Color Planning

How do you plan all this? When I plan color, I like to take samples of all the elements I will be using, assemble them on a table, take a good squint and see what comes out as an ensemble. By squinting you are looking at each separate piece as it will appear in a finished room, surrounded and influenced by all the other colors in it. By squinting you also erase the details and get down to the very essence of the colors in an ensemble—the way you will actually see them in your living room. This is an old trick that artists use and it works well for plain people too. You can take a cue from some scene that appeals to you—perhaps a long-remembered winter setting or a favorite print, or an historical picture. One of my favorite room scenes is the music room at the Royal Pavilion at Brighton, England. It was a fantastic Oriental combination of red and gold walls with a glorious turquoise Axminster rug that, alas, was destroyed. Or you can take your colors from a patterned fabric that you can't live without.

Using Color Samples

Samples of color are easy to come by. You don't need to beg your decorator friends for paint chips or bug your local paint dealer for color chips, although these are two simple and expedient methods you can use. Make your own samples by looking at magazines as an artist would. Forget the model's face in the fashion magazine, but tear out a patch of the green dress she is wearing because it's just the shade you were searching for. Don't read the text in the cigarette ad, but notice that the sky behind the figure on horseback is the exact color you wanted. Maybe the wine color of the jersey on the football player in a sports magazine or the color of the lettuce in the recipe section of a woman's magazine is just what you've been looking for!

Learn to look for color wherever it appears, no matter how unrelated it may be to your living room. The yellow of a traffic sign, the blue on that box of detergent or the green of a soap wrapper may be just right for you. Keep a file of marvelous colors derived from these many ready sources. This will be an important first step in assembling your scheme, but even more important is that it will teach you to see color as it influences your environment. Your eye will become trained to catch these color signals wherever you may be, making your visual life infinitely more pleasurable in the process.

There are many places to look for the paler, more subtle colors. Writing papers, for example, come in glorious shades of ivory, tints of color and whites of every description. Cardboard boxes are often helpful, and I've even used discarded book jackets and wrapping paper, although these often tend to be too glossy.

Once you have your colors assembled, begin to team up the ones that strike your fancy, keeping in mind whatever you plan to salvage from your present living room. It's a good idea to do this color planning right in the living room, because colors will appear vastly different under different lighting. Keep in mind that color affects your room in three major ways: as it influences space, as it relates to texture and as it shapes balance and scale. These basic guidelines will help you choose among many kinds of color paths.

Color and Space

Color and space form a natural alliance. Some colors recede, drawing the eye up, up and away. Pale colors and whites, for example, are great space stretchers, particularly if the ceilings, walls and floors all relate. But even if you have darker floors, white walls and ceilings will expand whatever square footage you have.

Dark or bright colors, on the other hand, contract space. An old design trick is to paint one short wall of a rectangular room in a bright color, keeping the other three walls white or off-white. The bright color advances toward the eye, moving the short wall forward and pushing the two longer walls at right angles to it away from the eye. This visually alters the proportions of the space by making it seem more square. A room that is too large can be made to seem more in proportion by painting the whole thing dark. If the ceiling is too high for the length and width of the space, a dark color can be useful in making it seem lower.

Color affects space beyond the visual parameter as well. The color of a room contributes a large part to its "look." A room painted a rust red color will appear warm and comfortable. It might not be appropriate for a living room in a tropical climate, but it would be highly successful in Chicago or New York or Kansas City, where long winter months would seem infinitely less oppressive in a cozy, rosy room.

In warmer climates, white and light, airy colors would seem more appropriate. A pale room with white, stuccoized walls, natural wicker furniture upholstered in white canvas, a large round glass top on a bleached wood pedestal, small, elegant brass lamps, green plants in natural straw or woven baskets and a few yellow pillows for accents will seem cool and refreshing to the eye.

Today there are no rules in design. With the development of total home air conditioning, regional differences are disappearing and so are color schemes based on climatic characteristics. I've seen red rooms in Florida that looked just dandy, and white rooms in Chicago that were as airy as if they had been devised in the Caribbean. But that doesn't diminish the importance of color; it is still the most important factor in creating the look or feeling that you want in your room.

Color and Texture

Color is itself affected by texture. The thicker or more emphatic the texture the more diminished the color will seem. Flat, glossy or smooth surfaces project a much brighter image. A red color in paint, for example, will be ever so much brighter than the same color in a carpet or even a velvet fabric. This is because the impact of the color is dissipated by breaking the surface up into higher and lower parts, consequently making the lower parts, or the parts farthest from the light, seem darker. Light and dark, or chiaroscuro (the word used to describe shadows and depths in the paintings of the fourteenth- and fifteenth-century Italian masters), thus has a decisive impact on color. When you are planning your scheme, it is wise to compare colors in the actual textures you plan to use. In that way you won't be surprised or disappointed when you get the real thing.

Getting samples of fabrics is not too difficult; most stores will give you a small cutting of fabric you are considering. Carpet dealers are not always that generous. If they don't happen to have extra three-by-five samples of the texture and color you are thinking of using, they aren't likely to cut one out of a roll of carpet for you, and you can hardly blame them. But you *can* take your paint and fabric samples to the carpet showroom. Just be sure to try to re-create the kind of light you have in your living room. The fluorescent lighting in most carpet showrooms bears little or no resemblance to the quality of the light in your home. Try to take the sample to the window and look at your color in real, not man-made daylight, by far the most accurate measure of pigment you can find.

Color and Balance

Color has another aspect when you plan a room. Just as color affects space, it also affects balance and scale. Let's look at scale and color first. We just talked about the effect of color on space, or how certain uses of color can visually alter the proportions of a given space. Scale is affected by color in the same way. A large piece of furniture in a bright color that is vastly different from its background will look much larger than if it were covered in the same color as its background; in other words, the bright color will bring a chair forward, whereas the similar color will cause it to recede. In this process, the chair becomes smaller as it recedes, larger as it is more pronounced. Any piece of furniture can be accentuated or diminished by using contrasting colors in this way.

Color affects the balance in any room as well. A small piece of furniture covered in an accent color and set against a neutral wall can balance a much larger piece, a love seat or even a small sofa that is covered in a color similar to the walls. Color can influence balance in another way—a bright accent color should be used throughout any living space. For example, a bright blue bowl on the coffee table will look sadly out of place in an otherwise neutral room of beiges, browns and wood tones. But add a couple of pillows in a similar blue and a bit of the same color in a print or poster on the wall and all of a sudden it looks just right.

The idea of balance in a room is very much like balance in the way you dress. It would be unlikely for you to wear a pale pink evening dress with matching shoes and bag and then add a bright green necklace. But if the green of the necklace matched the shoes or the bag, you might be able to pull the whole thing off. A single small note of an unrelated color cannot work as an accent; it must be planned as part of the overall scheme, no matter how limited the scale or size of the pieces are, in order for it to be a meaningful accent.

There is a kind of rhythm in the use of color. You must anticipate not only how the colors in your scheme will look with one another, but also *where* they will be stationed in your room. There is a simple system for experimenting with this. Using your floor plan, cut a tiny piece of the color you plan to use on each piece of furniture and paste it to the plan; if you use double-faced tape you can pull the piece off easily. Look at the plan as you would a painting. If the color is distributed about the room, you can be fairly sure you will have a rhythmic pattern, whereas if it is all clustered in one part of the plan, the room will look color-heavy in one part and uninteresting in the others.

How Many Colors to Use

Is there a special number of colors that should go in a room? I've been asked this question at least two hundred times. The answer I always give is simple. There are no limits to the number—a whole rainbow will work but it must be in a very subordinate role. An example would be the living room that is black, brown and white with a collection of multicolored pillows on the sofa. There may be twenty colors in this room, but the basic scheme is white, brown and black.

A good guideline is to restrict your major colors to three or four, with one or two predominant, and remember that white is indeed a color. Then develop a group of minor colors that are pigmented spin-offs of the majors. Take a room that has Egyptian red walls, an amber tan carpet and basic brown upholstery. These are the three major colors. A smaller chair might be covered in a leather that looks like the amber tan. Two mobile ottomans could be in a pattern that combines the red and brown. Occasional pillows can be in rust shades with others in moss green. A Tiffany lamp and a Chagall print combine reds and greens like these. The brass lamps are after all a derivative of the amber floor as is the sherry in the wine decanter on the glass coffee table! A white ceiling and woodwork are a sharp punctuation mark and lighten the room. Many books blend all these colors. This a multicolored room with an easily defined color scheme.

Remember that colors don't have to match anymore. The old days of dying fabrics to match or spending days searching for an exact combination are over, happily. We are much freer, less up-tight about colors. Today's designer

is looking for color families and groups, rather than replicas—a healthy attitude. In nature, which we are so ready to imitate, it's rare for any colors to match. Just think of the colors of spring flowers or of the leaves in the fall. There is scarcely a match anywhere, but it all works together.

The nicest part of color is the price. It is the least expensive way to decorate your home. A good strong paint color can take the place of thousands of dollars of expensive furnishings; white can expand space without knocking down walls; an accent wall can change the proportions of your room; and bits of bright color can create a rhythmic pattern that far surpasses a costly patterned fabric in effectiveness. That's why I'm a color freak—it's such fun to experiment and play with color and be relaxed about the cost.

 Windows

Windows can be almost as important as color and form in establishing the look of your room. A friend saw my living room for the first time recently and congratulated me for having made it modern. I was a bit surprised at first, until I realized that he meant that the architectural background had given my furniture a contemporary look.

Four tall windows and two French doors fill most of two walls, and I covered them in white matchstick bamboo roll-up shades. These are contained neatly within wooden frames painted white and attached to the outer edge of the window trim as an extra molding. The furnishings include a strictly modern sofa and a glass and chrome coffee table; a contemporary love seat with a pair of Chippendale armchairs; a few antique smaller pieces; a black grand piano; and lots of plants, antiques, modern lamps and accessories. But the simple window treatment had done its thing and converted all of these into a blend that is indeed essentially contemporary.

For so many centuries windows were little more than holes in the wall—sometimes quite literally—to allow light and sometimes air to enter a space. In the earliest days they also acted as protective devices because they allowed the folks inside to peer out and see when their enemies were approaching.

In homes or castles where the only source of heat came from a wood-burning fireplace or kitchen stove, windows were covered with fabric to keep out the cold. In the old days, too, night air was thought to be a carrier of plague, and many windows were barricaded with heavy wooden shutters as well as draperies to make them airtight.

A later development was the Venetian blind. These were used in elegant eighteenth-century city homes to take the place of shutters, which were thought to be "provincial" and rustic.

Another window covering we take for granted today, the shade, was actually developed as a shop sign which could be rolled down to advertise the product made or sold within when the shop was closed. (Obviously, everyone in town knew what the shop sold when the doors were open.) These shades were used in conjunction with draperies and shutters to provide protection from any exigency of climate or circumstance.

Science and technology have, of course, changed the physical relationship of our homes and the outdoors. We have developed central heating and insulated walls and Thermopane to deal with the cold and drafty rooms that plagued peasant and emperor alike, and we have air conditioning to help relieve the heat indoors in the summer in temperate climates or all year in tropical climates.

Thus, windows today have assumed more of a decorative function than a practical, protective one. How to treat the windows in your living room will be a very vital question as you design your room.

Windows As Backgrounds

One of the reasons why windows are so important is that they are *backgrounds* for forms. I use the word "form" to mean any of the things we have in our rooms, from a sofa to a sculpture. If you look up the word "background," you'll find that the dictionary defines it as "that which is back of anything and against which it is viewed." Unfortunately, most of us have a tendency to forget that windows are definitely part of the background in a room. They are the largest vertical elements in any space, and the eye is oriented toward any element at a right angle to the floor. Window treatments must be related, therefore, not only to the walls upon which they occur but also to the forms that are viewed against them and, of course, to the floor to which they join. Occasionally, someone gets carried away and treats windows as if they were objects to be revered in and of themselves, thus isolating them thoroughly from the design of the room as a whole.

Picture a modern living room with sliding glass doors for windows, which are covered with simple white vertical blinds matching the walls of the room. Obviously, these windows are a background. In an elegant Federal-style parlor furnished with antiques of the period, two tall windows and a pair of French doors leading to the garden have beige silk draperies with a matching fabric-covered valance, the fabric only a shade paler than the painted walls. These windows are also background. Although they are treated individually, they blend so perfectly with the walls that they melt into the background them-

selves. This is an ideal way to treat two widely separated windows without losing their sense of belonging to the wall. It is certainly a viable alternate to the wall-to-wall treatment, which would be less appropriate for the architecture of the room and the traditional furnishings as well as more expensive.

Windows As Accents

Windows can also be accents, and in many cases this is the preferable treatment. If the room is too long and narrow and the windows are at opposite, far ends, use a different bright color in decorating them. An unusual style or color will make them look closer to the eye, and thus alter the unfortunate proportions of the space. Another good occasion for accented windows is when there is very little else of any interest in the room—for example, where the furnishings are sparse and somewhat characterless. A pair of accented windows would go a long way to relieve the monotony of the space.

How do you accent a window? A good example is the Red Room at the White House. The walls are white and there is a lovely antique Aubusson rug on the floor in grays and beiges with reds, roses and touches of many other colors. The two tall and majestic windows, which look out over the Mall to the Washington Monument and then to the Capitol, are framed in crimson draperies of a finely woven mohair wool made especially for this famous room. The upholstery on the antique furniture is in the same red in silks and moiré fabrics as well as in off-whites. But the furniture itself, although very beautiful, is actually subordinate to the color arrangement of the room. The brilliant red draperies play against the white walls, drawing the eye up and out to the spectacular center of historical Washington. The contrast of the window covering to the wall is the accent.

Another kind of accent window is in a room I designed for a young couple who were just decorating their first living room and wanted it to look both intimate and sophisticated. We painted the walls deep marine blue and built two sets of plywood hinged screens, actually a pair of twelve-inch-by-eight-foot boards with finished edges, to flank each side of the windows instead of draperies or curtains. These were dimensions decided by the budget; only two sheets of four-by-eight plywood were necessary, as each sheet made two pair for each of the two windows. These were painted the same deep color as the walls. Covering the space from ceiling to floor, they helped give a feeling of verticality to the otherwise horizontal, low-ceiling room. Within the actual window opening, which was a typical three-by-five-foot size, I hung white vinyl window shades, pleated horizontally just like a paper fan, with nylon cording running through the pleats so that one could pull them up like a Venetian blind. These sparkling, washable white window coverings, which can give privacy and light control to the room, are the real accent in the otherwise deep blue room. They give a crisp, clean look to the space and relate happily to the white wicker and lacquer pieces in the room.

One of the advantages of this kind of design is that the whole room can be totally changed with a coat of paint, including the accent. If five years from now the owners decided to display the very good modern furniture they have begun to acquire, as well as a few antiques they couldn't resist, they could cover the blue (both walls and hinged panels) with white paint, and thus the white shades would become part of the background. If they still wanted an accent at the windows, the shades would remain white and the panels could be painted a color to work with the other colors in the room. Still a third option would be to keep the panels and walls white and accent the windows by changing the color of the shades to match one of the working colors of the room.

Different Kinds of Window Coverings

Windows are immensely versatile parts of any room, and they are particularly important in the living room, where they usually are more prominent or larger or more carefully located—or possibly more of a problem for any of the above reasons.

Remember that window coverings have three basic functions: they allow light and air to enter a room, they provide privacy from the outside for the inside and they can reveal a beautiful view or conceal the fact that there is none at all. The window covering you choose must meet one or all of these needs. And we have learned over the last decade to take our windows seriously—and individually. There are so many new and popular coverings that the only sensible system is to list each and then see how best they apply to the three basic functions of any window covering.

Matchstick Blinds

These are one of the most popular of today's coverings. Matchstick blinds are made of fine, thin sections of bamboo, strung together by many threads that run from the top to the bottom of the entire shade. The bamboo is left a delectable natural color or sprayed white. The blinds can be fitted to a spring roller just like a window shade if they do not cover a long or especially wide area. Most often they are fitted with a cord and pulley arrangement, concealed by a self-valance at the top, if you care about things like that, and thereby roll up from the bottom. Two attractive spin-offs of these are what I call tortoise bamboo, the burn-marked outer peel of the bamboo in irregular strips roughly three-eights of an inch wide, and the unburned, faintly greenish outer peel of the bark, which is cut into eighth-inch strips and strung up the same way. The white-sprayed bamboo blind has a very elegant look and can be combined with

the most formal of furnishings, whereas the natural matchstick or the tortoise or outer peel blind combines best with casual furnishings for a natural look. All of these diffuse the light in a splendid way, but they require a shade behind them to give you total privacy or light control.

Another roll-up window covering is woven wood shades. These come in narrow stained wood or painted slats interwoven with threads of various textures and colors. The threads and slats can be made to coordinate with the color scheme of your room or, if you insist on draperies, the colors in the pattern. Woven wood shades, the most expensive of the matchstick blind window coverings, can also be hung in vertical folds on a traverse rod, looking very much like a drapery.

Pleated Shades

Another new idea is the pleated look. This can be done with vinyl or fabric and looks for all the world like a fan made of your favorite fabric. In vinyl, it makes a practical but opaque covering, which will give privacy as well as light control. In cloth it can be made with the sheerest of fabrics or a heavier, lined version, providing less or more privacy as required.

Shutters

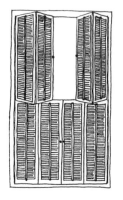

Shutters are one of the oldest window coverings known, although they are always popular. If you buy the unfinished version and install them yourself they will be less than half the cost of custom-made shutters, an extremely expensive window covering. Though the cost is high, it certainly does not exceed the price you would pay for traverse draperies with a sheer curtain beneath them, and for my money shutters are infinitely preferable. First of all, they accomplish the same degree of light control and privacy, but they still allow you to look out. They can be hinged totally back from the window for easy cleaning or more air, or they can be left in place and the louvers adjusted for light or privacy. Moreover, they can be divided horizontally into two or three units, so that the bottom part may be left closed while the upper part is drawn back. They can also be painted to match the walls or stained to match any wood in the room.

Shutter Panels

These flat sections consist of wood frames in side sections with movable louvers within the frame, just like a shutter. The difference is that the whole frame is attached by hardware at the top to a track, very much like a sliding closet door. Another version of this idea is the "plantation" shutter, a panel of thicker wood, hinged to one or more like sections and mounted on small casters for easier mobility. These can be used to flank a picture or plain window and simply rolled into place for more light control or privacy. Or they are left at the outer edges of the window, as you would a pair of drapery panels, with a window shade covering the actual glass of the window.

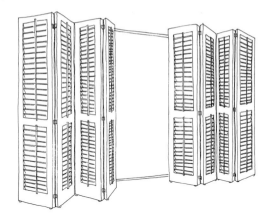

Screens

The logical next step is screens. These are solid pieces of plywood covered with paint or mirror or vinyl or fabric and used to take the place of drapery panels on either side of a window. They definitely require an additional covering for the window, unless you don't care about privacy or light control. Screens are versatile because they are reversible and can have a different color or pattern or treatment on the other side. They also provide a handy storage space behind for bulky, otherwise unstorable items, like a movie screen, for example.

Vertical Blinds

Vertical blinds are one of my favorite window coverings. They are adaptable to almost any kind of window, traversing the window just like a drapery on a tract mounted to the ceiling or the wall, and hanging to the floor or to the sill as needed. They can be made of any color or fabric, but my favorite is a simple

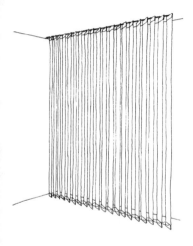

white shade cloth that can totally blacken a room if you rotate the louvers until they are flat. With a tiny flick of the cord you can allow brilliant sunlight to enter by rotating the louvers to another angle. For total sun penetration or a thorough window washing, pull them horizontally back toward the sides of the window. Verticals have another advantage over any other window covering; if a louver tears inadvertently, you have only to replace that one, rather than the entire set. It makes sense, when ordering these, to order a few extra louvers at the same time, just in case of an emergency.

Venetian Blinds

This old style window covering is truly versatile. You can use the currently fashionable mini-slat Venetians, with an almost invisible nylon cord to pull them up and down, or the reintroduced wood-stained version of the old wide slat blinds. You will find they are a totally functional covering, providing any degree of privacy and light or view control you may need. For those of you who may have had the tedious experience of cleaning Venetians, slat by slat, remember that air conditioning has taken most of the dust out of our living rooms and your job will have become negligible in the process.

Fabric Panels

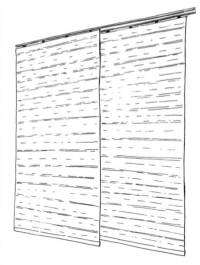

Another traversing device is fabric panels hung flat on a track made specially for this kind of treatment, with clamps to hold the panel instead of the usual hook-and-eye arrangement for traverse gathered draperies. The economy of this covering is obvious—it uses one-third the amount of yardage required for its pinch-pleated cousin. Another advantage is that if you choose a washable fabric, it is no problem at all to wash and press flat before rehanging. These panels can be hung on two or three parallel tracks and used in the full width of the fabric for the most economic versions. An opaque fabric would give total privacy of course, but a translucent, lacy fabric looks gorgeous.

Window Shades

By far the most underrated window covering is the good old shade. Simple in concept, inexpensive and easy to install yourself, requiring almost no maintenance, shades are beginning to become popular all over again. Today's shades are a bit different from the ivory or dark green versions of the last generation. They come in a variety of stock fabrics, textures, colors and even patterns. There are shades that have a self-laminating surface to which you can paste your own fabric, or shades with a smooth surface that you can paint on yourself. And there is no limit to what you can do with borders and pulls. In other words, shades are in largely because many folks today just don't want to bother with the expense and maintenance of costly, elaborate window coverings. Shades also blend with other window coverings, like shutters or screens.

How to Choose Your Window Covering

All these window coverings, though varying immensely in style and cost, have one thing in common. They require little or no maintenance, unlike draperies or curtains, which often cost about one-third of their purchase price to have dry-cleaned and rarely look as good afterward. There are windows, of course, that do require curtains. Heavy draperies are excellent insulators against cold or drafts, and they deal effectively with large glass areas today when heating is expensive. And there are still some folks who need the one-quarter inch of "softness" of draperies at the window. But to make any of these window coverings work for you, you must design them into your own living room. Look at your windows and try to choose a covering that matches both your lifestyle and your décor.

Are you one of those people who likes to have an enormous amount of light by day, but needs to control the light to keep direct sun from fading a delicate fabric or a set of valuable drawings inside the room. A heavy drapery is probably not the answer to your problem, because it allows either full light or no light at all to enter the room. A more flexible system would be a window covering that allows varying degrees of light to enter. A Venetian blind is the least expensive answer, and from there you can go up the price ladder to vertical blinds and to shutters. All of these are what I call "integral" window coverings—one covering does everything for the window, whether it is for good looks or plain light control. Venetians and shutters adapt most successfully to separated, conventionally shaped windows, and both are exceptionally adept at light control. Vertical blinds will also adapt to a small window, but since they move horizontally on a traverse rod, just like a drapery, they will do well with a picture window as well. How they will look in your room is for you to determine.

Plain Venetian blinds, for example, will look a bit unfinished in a pair of separated three-by-five windows. But if you trim the frames with a six-by-six-inch box of stock lumber, stained dark to match your walnut-stained floors, then plain white mini-slat blinds will look smashing. Try the reverse, as I did in a living room with two plain-jane windows. I trimmed them from the ceiling to the floor with a one-by-four-inch wood frame, thin edge facing out. Then I hung wide-slat wood Venetians in a dark walnut finish just like the elegant highboy that stands between the two windows, running the blinds from the ceiling to the floor.

Still another very satisfying treatment for single, separated windows are shutters. These can look marvelous even if they are fitted within the existing window frame and simply painted the color of the walls or a contrasting color. Shutters, moreover, can effectively disguise different types of windows. You've all seen the living room with two separated windows and one door leading to the patio or garden. I designed a living room with this very arrangement, by framing all three openings with a two-by-two frame, painted white like the walls, from the ceiling to the floor. The frame had two uses. The first was to make all three openings the same shape, because the windows were smaller than the door and they stopped short of the floor by about thirty inches. The second use was to give me a strong base for hanging the shutters.

Shutters were an ideal choice, because they divided the window space in two vertically. The thirty-inch space below the window remains closed, concealing the fact that the windows do not go to the floor, and one of these lower sections conceals a below-the-window air conditioner. The upper section, covering the glass, opens easily to let light and air in. The shutters at the door are a single pair, opening all the way to reveal the outdoors but continuing up to the same height as the windows. This simple covering of white-painted shutters looks marvelously at home with a combination of fine French furniture and sleek modern chrome and steel, polished wood floors, a thick shaggy off-white flokati area rug and hanging ferns and a tall tree at the windows.

Suppose you have a picture window but no view at all? This is one of the most common problems with today's living room, largely because builders often place the house so that the living room picture window faces the street. Why this is done remains a mystery, but as a result, you can drive up any residential street in this country and see hundreds of homes with picture windows facing nothing more than moving cars. Is it any wonder that the average homeowner places a large lamp on a large table in front of this piece of awkwardly placed glass and calls it a day by drawing the draperies? If you're stuck with this unhappy arrangement, skip the lamp and the table and think *inside.* Your best bet is a window covering that will conceal the cars and give you a bit of privacy in the evening as well.

A good choice for this would be vertical blinds. In a living room I worked on, with a large picture window facing the street, I used white vertical blinds made of a heavy-duty shade cloth which totally blocks light and assures complete privacy. During the day, the louvers can be opened to allow sun and air into the room, keeping a big garden growing in place of the usual table and lamp. The garden is actually a large, shallow box on concealed casters, with a galvanized liner fitting neatly and inconspicuously inside. Plain white gravel, which reflects the sunlight up onto the leaves of the plants, also retains the necessary humidity for the plants. A large *Ficus exotica* (tropical fig) tree is surrounded by dense lower plants, all of these standing in their own pots which are happily concealed by the combined foilage and the frame of the garden.

The advantage of a mobile garden like this is that it can be moved from one part of the large window to the other, to take maximum advantage of the dif-

ferent angles of the sun at different times of the year. An antique deck chair and a tiny lacquer chest keep this area company, and it is a marvelously private place to read or sew or just think without looking at cars. The leafy foliage blurs the straight lines of the vertical louvers to give the "soft" look we seem to need for large glass areas.

I designed a window covering for a living room in a modern high-rise apartment house. The apartment was on the seventeenth floor, and there were no neighboring buildings as high, so privacy was not a requirement. However, the extremely hot afternoon sun was hard on the pale pastel colors of a cluster of silken pillows on the sofa. To offset this harsh light, I hung four fabric panels on a track which was attached to the ceiling just like any drapery track, about four inches from the glass itself. The fabric panels were made of felt cut out in a geometric pattern of small squares. When this is hung flat at the window it looks like modern lace, yet it is enough to diffuse and deflect the direct sunlight at the window. Another big advantage of felt is that it does not need to be hemmed on the sides. One hem at the top and one at the bottom for the rods that hold the fabric taut is all the stitching you will need to do, and if you have a sewing machine you can easily make these yourself.

But perhaps you're one of the lucky ones who has a picture window with a perfectly lovely view. In one room I worked on there was no need for privacy or light control—the furnishings were a collection of natural textures, relatively unaffected by the sun, and there was no one nearby to worry about. The room had three tall windows on one wall. I trimmed these in dark wood on three sides, to contrast with a white burlap wall covering and to carry vertically the look of the dark wood floors. To the thick wood trim I attached many Lucite brackets from which I hung plants of many varieties in baskets at different heights, simply adding chain to those I wanted lower. Tall and low clusters of plants on the floor joined the hanging baskets to soften the strong verticality of the wood trim and to diffuse the equally strong light from the uncovered glass, providing a growing window covering that brings great pleasure to its owner.

Windows have a way of falling into typical patterns. With today's infinitely versatile and inexpensive coverings, you should be able to create attractive window treatments like those described above, without making too much of a dent in your furnishing budget.

Remember that heat requirements and privacy accounted for, there's no more perfect window covering than none at all. After all, why invest in all that glass just to cover it up? But being realistic is part of good interior design, and some diffusion of the sun's direct rays through your window may be required.

A BAKER'S DOZEN TRICKS FOR WINDOWS

- An inexpensive way to frame a window is to use a lambrequin, which is defined by Webster as a ''short decorative, hanging pendent from a shelf or from the casing above a window, hiding the curtain fixtures.'' In my private lexicon, it is no longer just fabric but a box frame that fits around the top and two sides of any window. With this device, you can make a small window seem larger and more important, by making the lambrequin large—a foot wide, for instance— you can visually alter the proportions of the real window. The frame can be painted to match the surrounding walls or covered with fabric.

- Use shades as a background for do-it-yourself murals. For instance, I used beige shades in a smooth finish against white walls. On three side-by-side shades in a picture window I painted diagonal stripes, about one inch thick, in white acrylic paint, (use parallel bands of masking tape to keep the lines straight). The stripes angled up on two shades and down on one, so that when the shades are all hanging at the same length, the mural has the effect of a modern landscape. If the shades are pulled to different heights, as is so often the case, the whole wall becomes an abstract mural.

- Another inexpensive but effective technique is to add a decorative border to the hem of your shade. For a room with a ''natural'' look, buy a two-inch-wide bamboo rod (available in lumberyards or drapery workrooms) and have it split in half the long way. Glue it together with the hem of the shade fitting neatly between the halves. Or buy a one-inch pole, leave it in one piece and staple the hem of the shade to the back of the pole to hide the hem and the staples. Other alternatives include beaded hems for Victorian rooms, or vinyl mylar (a mirrorlike material available in upholstery shops) strips for shades in modern rooms.

- Shade pulls are fun to experiment with. Try using tennis balls (or ping-pong balls for smaller shades) in day-glow colors in bright contemporary rooms with white walls and white shades. Napkin rings come in many odd materials and make handsome shade pulls for very little cash. I've used napkin rings made of snail shells in a living room at the seashore and used straw wrapped rings in the city. If you're ambitious you can make needlepoint pulls in any shape to match the colors of your room. For really low-budget pulls, use the simple wooden curtain rings, about three inches in diameter, painted white or red or any color that works with your shades and your room.

- Shades that pull up from the bottom of the window can provide even more eye interest. Buy shades in fantastic, bright colors, like blue and green, and use them in side-by-side windows with one going up and one going down. Getting shades to pull up is easy. You need a fastener at the midpoint of the window on the upper sash, and a loop on the shade that hooks on to this to keep it up. If you want to adjust your bottom pull-up shade, you need a slightly more complicated device which any shade or drapery dealer can help you install or which you can find out about at any shade shop. If you have three side-by-side windows, or a picture window wide enough for three or four shades, you can vary these patterns using three colors and ending up with a window that has the effect of a modern geometric painting.

- Fabric stretched across an unattractive window is another inexpensive way to disguise its proportion and make it more important. This can be done at home by just about anyone with a hammer, nails and stapler. Make two frames of one-by-one stock lumber in rectangles or squares to fit the width of your window, the heights to be determined by how you wish to change the height of the window. Buy a couple of yards of fabric with a pattern that works in your room, and wrap the frames with the fabric, stretching it tightly and stapling it to the back of the frame. Now attach these to your window frame, setting them far enough apart to provide light and air and room to raise and lower the windows. With this device, you can make a pair of short, squat windows appear tall and graceful without spending too much effort or money on the solution. The nicest part of these frames is that you can change the fabric whenever you get tired of the pattern.

- If you're the kind of person who really digs shutters but can't afford them, try just shuttering the lower half of a double-hung window. Attach the shutter to the outside of the window frame with hinges so that it can be opened or closed. The shutters should reach up to just above the horizontal sash in the middle of the window, thus concealing the mechanism and making a neater look. This will usually give you enough privacy, and if the shutter is painted the same color as the walls surrounding it, it will look like part of the architecture, rather than the skimpy half it really is. A hanging plant basket attached to a long hook at the top of the window frame will fill the empty half very nicely, giving a finished look to the window and making the half-height shutter seem more logical.

- If you hate anything but washable curtains but don't think curtain fabric will look right in your room; how about toweling? Terry cloth comes by the yard, as well as in towels, although I have no objection whatever to making towels into curtains if the size is appropriate.

- Skipping window coverings altogether and simply working with the glass itself is another inexpensive method. If you like stained-glass windows, you can convert conventional clear glass by using translucent tissue paper in glowing colors. Overlap the edges of the paper to get shades of still more color, using Elmer's or any white glue. Try tearing the paper for even more dramatic effects. You can create different geometric shapes, like a large, abstract flagstone pattern, using three or four shades of tissue in a family of colors, like oranges, yellows and pale lemon and peach. Tissue-paper stained glass is a marvelous system for eliminating an unattractive view, providing privacy and giving glow to your room even if you have a northern, sunless exposure.

• Still another way to treat the glass itself is to use masking tape. Buy a few rolls of the smooth white variety or the ordinary tan masking type in a two-inch width and make diagonal stripes on your windows. For a pair of side-by-side windows, for instance, the diagonals on the top pair of glass sections could run opposite one another slanting down, and the diagonals on the bottom pair could run slanting up to create a huge diamond pattern from the paired windows. Keep the taped lines as close together as you want, still allowing light to pass through. Similar giant patterns can be made with concentric squares or rectangles. The best part of taped windows is that it's easy to vary the pattern or allow less or more light to enter, depending on your need or the season of the year.

• Traverse rods can be a great help to anyone who wants to try new twists on old themes. There are special clamp attachments to fit traverse rods so that you can hang panels instead of the traditional drapes. The lightweight kind are available at any hardware or drapery shop and can be used to hang fabric panels or other light materials.

• A heavier clamp on a traverse rod can be used to hang plexiglas panels instead of fabric. In a modern city living room with a window wall looking out on a small terrace, I used two heavy-duty traverse rods with clamp attachments. I bought two panels of four-by-eight-foot clear plexi in a soft gray tint and clamped them to the rods. I had a finger-size hole cut into each panel at doorknob height to move them back and forth so as to ward off sticky fingerprints. If you need privacy, you could buy the translucent rather than the clear plexi. It also comes in varying degrees of translucence in white.

• Still another way to take advantage of the versatile traverse rod is to hang it with plant baskets and lots of floating, drooping ferns or ivies. Use bits of chain to extend some of the plants below others so that they are hanging at many levels. The best part of this type of arrangement is that the pots can be moved to change patterns simply by sliding the hook along the rod. Place more ferns on floor pedestals of various heights, making a beautiful greenhouse out of the bay window. A good way to make this marvelous greenery seasonal is to set a few flowering plants into the group. In the summer, for example, exchange a fern or two with a hanging basket of bright pink fuchsia or yellow lantana, and in the winter flowering chrysanthemums on the pedestals (or gardenias or poinsettias at Christmas time), making your window the focal point of your living room.

Floors

Like windows, floors can be either background or accent. In fact, it is easier to visualize floors as backgrounds and accents than windows. We are used to thinking of floors in these static terms, and there are far fewer options in floor-covering styles than windows because of maintenance factors. Window coverings must be maintainable, of course, but no one walks on them. This means that there is a very limited range to the type of fabric one can apply to a floor, although there is, to be sure, tremendous variety within this range.

It is only recently that we have begun to understand the versatility of floors and to recognize the tremendous decorative potential of that flat, horizontal surface in the living room that people took for granted for so many generations. Even today there is a reluctance to spend the proportionate amount per square foot on floor coverings that we spend on furniture or even window treatments, or for that matter on our body fashion. For openers, just think that a woman will balk at spending $159.95 for a handsome rug that she might use daily for ten years, but she would hardly think twice about buying a coat for that amount, a garment she might use fifty times before giving it away. A handkerchief costs more per square inch than a carpet.

Carpeting

Today there are carpets for every pocketbook. In fact, manufacturers have improved the styling and color of machine-made carpets to such an extent that it is often difficult to tell an expensive from an inexpensive wall-to-wall fabric. In area rugs also, modern machine-made "Orientals" look so good that unless you are the biggest snob in town there is no reason at all why you cannot use one of these beauties in your parlor.

Floor coverings were about the earliest furnishing devised for the home. We know from excavations that skilled weavers were creating rugs of exquisite Oriental design as long as 2,500 years ago. Nomadic people herded the sheep, sheared, spun and dyed their wool and then wove it into thick sturdy rugs that covered the floors and walls of their tents. The rugs were also used to form a sitting area over thick cushions—the forerunner of the carpeted conversation "pit" of the modern home.

Hundreds of years of development in yarn quality, weaving, dying and creating pattern took place before our modern carpeting or rugs could be produced. The masterful Savonnerie and Aubusson rugs developed in France in the sixteenth century were a gigantic step forward in the refinement of pattern and color in floor coverings. No nuance of color was overlooked, no detail was too tiny for these master weavers. The tapestries they created took the place of paintings and they were able to translate any painting into a rug. Indeed, rugs, paintings and upholstery for chairs and settees were frequently all designed together in the sixteenth and seventeenth centuries to make a single pattern statement for a room—a concept that we have often seen adapted to the modern living room.

In later developments, the big machine-powered looms of England brought the Wilton and Axminster construction to the manufacture of floor coverings, paving the way for the wall-to-wall carpeting that is very much the same in every way as the carpet we use today. Recently, the tufting machine has been added to the arsenal of hardware of the carpet mill. Tufting is less expensive than weaving because the yarn does not actually interweave with the backing; it merely pierces it. Tufting is also considerably faster, allowing mills to turn out a great deal more yardage per day and requiring fewer people to work and supervise the manufacturing process.

The history of carpets and floor coverings is an interesting one, paralleling as it does the major social and scientific advances in world history.

The most important things you should know about carpet and rugs are related to their construction, texture and fiber content.

Carpet Construction

The construction of the modern carpet falls into two major categories—woven and tufted. Although woven carpet seems to hold up better in heavy traffic areas in commercial usage, a good quality tufted carpet will work just as well in any area of the home, and it is likely to be a bit less expensive. Tufting machines today have been built to create patterns almost as intricate as those produced by looms, and unless you are looking for a very complex and expensive patterned rug or carpet, a tufted quality will do just as well. The major facts you should know about either a tufted or woven carpet are its density and its pile height.

Density

Density, measured by the number of stitches per inch, is the most important fact to understand about carpet construction. You don't have to painstakingly measure and compare an inch of any carpet you are considering, just fold it back on itself. If a great deal of the backing shows (carpet people call this "grin," because it looks like a smile breaking out), the density may leave something to be desired. A closely tufted or woven carpet or rug will be dense enough to withstand many years of wear, regardless of the pile height. Although a carpet is measured by face weight, total weight and pile height, density is still the major consideration in choosing one for your home.

Pile Height

A great many folks think that a high-pile carpet looks more expensive. Actually, there are a great many high-pile carpets (which means only that the yarn length on the face of the carpet is longer) that are relatively inexpensive because they are rather loosely woven. These will not do at all on hard-wear areas, because the yarn flattens out when you step on it.

A densely woven or tufted low-pile carpet is an excellent investment for a living room that has a fixed traffic pattern or is geared to constant family use. It is also a good quality for any part of your parlor where you serve food because a low, closely woven rug or carpet is easier to clean. A loosely woven, high-pile carpet or rug can be perfectly at home in a parlor that is off the beaten path, where it is used more for guests and grownups than for children and dogs, or where there is another room for rough daily use.

Carpet Texture

Texture is the second major factor in choosing the proper carpet for your living room. There are four major types of textures and each has its own properties and propensities for wear and tear.

Plush

The most popular texture is plush, a woven or tufted material with all the loops formed in the manufacturing process sheared at the same height. Probably the only reason why some people don't like plush is that it shows footprints, in what I call "pools." These are shadings where the uppermost face of the yarn is depressed by constant wear. I like these pools; they give light and shadow which creates texture in an otherwise bland surface. Besides, I like the idea that the carpet does not look perfect or new, but rather a part of the household, reflecting its use.

Because the loops are cut, plush does not have the resiliency or resistance to soil that a tightly woven loop quality will give you. It does give a feeling of elegance that no other texture can provide, and it is particularly appropriate to living rooms that are set somewhat aside from a regular traffic pattern and to rooms that have a formal look.

I used plush in a room that features a pair of authentic French eighteenth-century open-arm chairs covered in a delicious floral of pale greens, ivories and deep rust red on a peach background. The chairs are beside a simple contemporary sofa in an ivory twill. Some of the pillows on this sofa are made of the same fabric pattern as the chairs, and others are made in solid colors from the print. A high-back wing chair in russet leather and a creamy travertine cubed coffee table complete the seating group. The background is just as lush. The windows are covered in shutters painted ivory to match the chair rail and woodwork; the walls are painted in a slightly paler peach than the background color of the fabric; and the carpet, like a rich ground, is a pale rust plush. This color works with the peach, blends with the rust of the leather and the print and acts as a stage to set off the elegant lines of the furniture and accessories. Somehow, plush was the only texture that would have worked in this room, with its beautiful furniture and subtle colors.

Shag

Shag is exactly the opposite from plush. It has an informal, rough and ready look and seems to work best with modern furniture. The shaggy bear look of this type of carpet would seem downright odd with fine French furniture, while it is perfectly at home with Early American or modern. Shag is made the same way as plush. In other words, it is tufted in high loops. These loops are then cut through with a shearing knife, to make the shaggy ends that give it its thick, lush look. It differs from plush in its looser density and longer yarn ends.

Shag comes in many densities. The less tightly the yarn is packed, the more the ends are likely to lie down flat—a typical problem with shag rugs or carpets. Some stores even sell shag "rakes" designed to fluff up the rugs and keep the pile even, very much like combing your hair. Some shags, particularly

those made with nylon fiber, which is a good deal bulkier than wool, polyester or acrylic yarns, withstand traffic and wear. But almost all shags are likely to be a gigantic pain in the neck unless you decide that you like the way they look in their up-and-down worn circumstances. Then you can spend your time on more constructive pastimes than raking your rug.

Because of the long yarn length, shag is very difficult to clean and should be used in living rooms where food is not habitually served, where the room is not a constant traffic path and only if your dog is house-trained.

In a small living room I worked on, I used a shag carpet in an off-white natural color and painted the walls the same off-white, the color of a piece of old writing paper. The other background feature was a large glass picture window, and I covered this with vertical blinds on a traverse rod, in the same off-white natural linen as the walls. This background was to be an all-white shell for a fantastic collection of African primitive wood carvings, so I covered a love seat and two small armchairs in natural Haitian cotton. I used the Mies van der Rohe Barcelona coffee table, a marvel in chrome and glass that I myself have owned for ten years and never tired of, and flanked it with two classic steel-framed Wassily chairs with seat and back slings in white cotton canvas. In this elegant whitish room, which might otherwise seem cold and forbidding, the shag rug works a miracle by giving the room enough texture to make it look warm and inviting without destroying the look of the space, a space that no other texture would have fit as properly.

For those of you who like the shag look but can't cope with the comb, I would suggest that happiest compromise, a shag area rug. One of the most popular of these, the Greek flokati rug, is dense wool closely woven in a luscious natural white. There are credible copies available now in acrylic yarn, a bit easier to clean and definitely less expensive. Just plain ordinary shag in an off-white can be super in a living room with a dark-stained and polished wood parquet floor, in the proper size to delineate the sitting furniture and acting as an invitation to be sociable. Shags do indeed come in any color you desire. You might try a deep chocolate brown or charcoal gray area rug if you want something practical, or even a rich rust red or deep sea blue. Any of these would be smashing on a white vinyl tiled floor or even on a wood floor finished in its natural light color.

Shag Plush

A final compromise on shag is the shag plush, a kind of happy medium between the flat look of plush and the overgrown look of shag. Shag plush has a rough textured look that works well with either a modern or contemporary room or a room filled with Provincial or wicker furniture. This type of rug is constructed so that the yarn is longer than plush, but of a heavier ply, or diameter and more dense, so that it does not crush at the drop of a footstep like

shag. Because it has the texture of shag, however, it also doesn't "pool" like plush.

I used shag plush in a living room in an old Victorian home; dark woodwork and a highly decorated plaster ceiling gave this room a librarylike atmosphere, perfect for the book-loving family living in it. I lined the walls with bookshelves stained to match the woodwork, doors and window trim, and fitted the windows with wood Venetian blinds in the same dark wood tone as the shelves and woodwork. The walls that showed around windows and doors were painted white. I used a new paint that has a stuccolike texture, very appropriate for the Victorian period. Stucco was in heavy use at the end of the nineteenth century when walls were not made of smooth gypsum board, and the stucco thus covered a multitude of cracks and imperfections.

I used a contemporary modular seating group, basically two sofas that turned corners to create a spacious U-shape around a marvelous coffee table made from a light oak Victorian kitchen table with a heavy pedestal base cut down to coffee table height and stained dark. The carpet and the upholstery are the same shade of pearl gray. Bold dark brown and off-white batik fabric in many similar patterns covers a cluster of fat occasional pillows, which are the only patterns other than the many books in this cozy room, where the heavily textured carpet makes everything soft and sumptuous.

Loop

The most serviceable quality of carpet manufactured today is the loop. Low-level loops form a dense, impregnable flooring, and the round tops of the loops prevent easy staining. The tensile strength of the fiber is also strongest in loops, especially in the continuous filament yarn into which nylon fibers are made. Thus there is an infinity of yarn with no loose ends that gives strength and stability to the carpet.

The heavily trafficked areas in your home should have looped carpet, either level loops or the equally popular multilevel version in which there are some high and some low loops. The obvious advantage is that footprints and soil show a good deal less on these. A tightly woven loop would do best, for example, in a heavily trafficked living room where the only way to get through the house from the door to other rooms is through this space. Other parts of your home might benefit as well; multilevel or level loops do well in family rooms, on stairs and even in the kitchen.

I worked on a home where the front door opened directly into the living room. From this door, there was a clear path to the dining room and the kitchen, a favorite route for the family's three young children, not to mention a bouncy boxer dog. I decided on a dense, tightly tufted low-level loop in a deep rust, not dark enough to show white footprints from the dusty outdoors, yet dark enough to conceal most of everything else. The furniture was divided into two groups, to provide for a diagonal path to the dining room. One cluster is a

low, round marble-topped table and three swivel chairs in an off-white plastic that looks so much like leather that even the cow wouldn't know the difference.

The other seating group is oriented to the fireplace and includes a fabulous Victorian settee, the one-armed sexy style that is so hard to find, that I discovered in a country flea market. Covered with deep peach felt, the settee is placed opposite the fireplace at a right angle to the long wall and is flanked by two Italian open-arm chairs in natural ash with textured woven rush seats. Completing this group is a square, glass-topped coffee table on a cube painted to match the carpet, making the table top seem to float effortlessly above the floor. Two mirrored pedestals for plants reflect a lot of the color and texture of the carpet as well. Textured scorched bamboo roll-up shades cover the tall windows from ceiling to floor. The walls are painted a pale tan bamboo color, a good background for the furniture and for a garden of cacti of different species and sizes in natural wicker baskets. The carpet color unites the two separate groups in this lovely room.

Patterned Carpets

All these textures come in patterns as well as solids. The easiest texture to pattern is plush, the traditional background for Oriental rugs. New techniques, however, have made it possible to create tiny geometric patterns, in a variety of colors and sizes, in a tightly looped texture. Shags are easy to tuft in large-scale nonrepetitive patterns, similar to the traditional Scandinavian rya rug. Patterns can even be printed on flat, dense fabrics.

Choosing a pattern depends on the look you want. An Oriental rug is a practical and handsome addition to almost any room. From it can be derived the colors for the upholstery and walls, and it can be used to bring a seating group together in a prescribed area of the room.

The tiny new geometrics look marvelous in wall-to-wall carpeting. They have a disciplined, chic look that can be a lively background for a room full of furniture, yet they are just as practical as Orientals and less costly. If you don't like the wall-to-wall look but you do like small patterns, you can have your carpet dealer make you an area rug of a mini-pattern and then fringe or bind the ends with the major color of the pattern.

Shag area rugs are lush and fun and no longer expensive. A thick shag pattern, in a Moroccan or American Indian design, can establish a mural-like effect on the floor but you must be careful not to compete with it on the walls. In a living room with a patterned shag, paint the accent wall in a color taken from the rug design to bring the two perpendicular elements together. A shaggy patterned rug can make a beautiful work of art hung on the wall itself.

Carpet Fibers

Carpet fibers may sound confusing, but if you reduce them to essentials, they're easy to remember. There are four generic families in carpet: wool, acrylic, nylon and polyester. All the brands and trade names fall into one of these four families. All these fibers can be woven or tufted, and they are available in any of the textures I have described. There are also some chic alternates, like braided or knotted cotton, or sisal and hemp in squares of the woven broadloom variety.

What fiber is best for you? Use a bit of elementary knowledge and a lot of common sense to make your fiber choice. Nylon is the strongest fiber made, but the average living room does not really require maximum fiber strength unless you have an army in hobnailed boots living at home. Nylon is less expensive than wool or acrylic carpet, but it doesn't adapt as easily to color or texture or pattern. Although it is also relatively easy to soil, nylon is much easier to clean than the other fibers. Polyester is the least costly fiber. It soils easily and does not clean as well as nylon, but it comes in a rainbow of many brilliant hues, accepting dyes more readily than nylon. Acrylics accept dye well, cost more than nylon or polyester and soil less readily than either. They do not clean as well as nylon but they feel better and have more bulk and lushness than polyester if you're after that look. Wool is, of course, the Cadillac of fibers; it is the most expensive and it can adapt to any dye or detail of pattern or texture. It is subject to moths and mildew and, being a natural fiber, is easy to soil and harder to clean than man-made fibers.

Other Floor Coverings

Of course, there are floor coverings other than carpets or rugs. There are fantastic parquet wood floors or plain old-fashioned oak strips in light or dark stained finishes. Wood floors have a natural elegance and richness that no other floor covering can approximate, as well as a marvelous feel if you're wild about going barefoot like I am. A small shag area rug or an Oriental on a highly polished wood floor has a look so unique that nothing can quite compare. It produces an effect that is equally handsome and at home with modern or traditional furniture, with fine authentic pieces or just junk. Wood floors work as well in a living room with navy blue walls and rugged cotton and canvas upholstery as they do with white stucco walls and a brilliantly colored paisley fabric.

There are imitations of wood that work well for folks who like the look but cannot afford the real thing. Vinyl wood comes in strips, parquet and tiny squares in plain patterns or herringbones. Vinyl can be made to look like anything from flagstone to brick to octagonal terra cotta tiles. Vinyl comes in small modules or in sheets and is remarkably easy to maintain. Although it does not have the richness or patina of the natural products, it is a happy compromise if you are not after the wall-to-wall look of carpeting. I've used vinyl brick floor covering in a grayed white in a room with deep brown walls and two majestic peacock chairs flanking an armless sofa created of huge fluffy pillows in natural cotton canvas and supported by a brown lacquered frame. A series of brown chalk sketches on white paper are framed in chrome on the wall above the pillows. For the windows I used white shades with a chrome pull strip that came from an auto repair shop across the bottom. The chrome finish was repeated in two pharmacist's floor lamps and a giant mirror cube for a coffee table, reflecting the bricks over and over. Plants in natural clay pots stand on the floor by the twin windows, making the brick look like a greenhouse floor in contrast to the sophisticated effect of the chrome and the dark walls.

How to Choose Your Floor Covering

No matter what you use for your floors—vinyl or any of the man-made resilient floorings, wood, carpet or area rugs—no matter the texture or the fiber, your floor covering is designed to do one of three major things for your room. It can extend space, it can bring space together and it can provide an accent. To make a sensible decision for your living room, you should decide in advance which of these vastly different functions you want your floor covering to serve.

In a small room that you desperately want to enlarge visually, either wall-to-wall carpeting or a wood or vinyl floor will help to extend the space, particularly if the floor and wall work together in color. For the tiniest living room I ever saw, I used a wheat beige plush carpet, painted the walls a slightly lighter shade and the ceiling an off-white. A travertine marble mantle combined the two shades and also became the focal point for the seating group. This group consisted of a Chippendale camel-back two-seater covered in a beige and white twill opposite two country French chairs with their frames bleached to the color of the travertine and with white linen upholstery. Between the chairs is a coffee table made from a tree trunk of the same bleached wood shade as the chair frame, polished and barkless and covered with a clear round glass top. The room is further enlarged by using mirrored hinged panels on either side of the French doors that are the windows of the room and that lead to a glorious garden. In midwinter, thin translucent off-white curtains are set into the window frames on traverse rods, to be drawn when the sun sets. The carpet joins the walls and the upholstery to extend and stretch the space, all of these elements repeated and further extended in the mirrors.

As a sharp contrast, a patterned area rug can be the focus for a room, whether by color or pattern or size. I designed a city living room for a couple who wanted it to have country chic. The floors were stained in deep brown to match the heavy woodwork trim around six windows on facing sides of the room. Within the deep-set window I put shutters to match the floor and trim, giving an English men's club look to the room.

For the dark stained floor I chose a splendid Moroccan area rug, with a huge thick braided fringe. The rug is natural off-white with a saddle russet diamond in a traditional African design. It is large enough for the two sofas that face one another at right angles to the fireplace wall, which is painted in stucco-finish white, with the texture enriched by a light track overhead. The sofas are contemporary, upholstered in saddle leather, and are accompanied by two French pull-up chairs covered in navy wool. The area rug holds all these pieces together, plus a modern coffee table and, behind one of the sofas, a handsome Parsons table on which sits a pair of elegant table lamps with navy blue and white Chinese ceramic bases. Two chrome floor lamps illuminate the other sofa and work with the table base and the finish of the overhead track lights. The entire color scheme and the location of the seating group is given focus by the size and color of the pattern of the Moroccan rug. Just try to imagine this room without it.

Floors can bring a room together as nothing else in it can, because they are the single largest uninterrupted part of any room. In some rooms I've worked on, including my own living room, the owners have had so many disparate and diverse furnishings that using the floor is the only way to get it all back together. In one room I designed for a country home that dates back to before the Civil War, I used the floor to unify the furnishings. The furniture was marvelous: a pair of Chippendale chairs in a very dark finish, a simple flared-arm sofa in white upholstery, a pair of spool-back chairs in maple bleached to a very light finish and a Hepplewhite game table in the same light finish. A huge Chinese screen in blacks, browns, golds and russets dominated the space, and dark but whimsical ancestor portraits hung over the mantel and sofa. The light and dark furniture was charming, but it seemed to belong to two separate living rooms. To unify it, I chose a wood floor. But instead of one finish I used two, running dark and light colors in alternating stripes across the length of the rather long room. The floor, though brand-new and contemporary in its bold stripe, somehow manages to work with the off-white walls and the tremendous variety of styles and finishes of the furnishings. It brings them all together like a good painting where the many features are all part of a grand scheme that makes you sit back and enjoy being part of it.

Floors can be a major part of your living room. Think of them in terms of their three principal functions, as unifiers, as accents and as extenders, before you decide on your floor covering. Then choose the one that works best for you and meets the needs of your lifestyle.

A BAKER'S DOZEN TRICKS FOR FLOORS

- If you like the idea of a multilevel living room, build a plywood box about eight inches above the floor at one end of the room, and carpet this platform, making it the focus of the room. Or actually carve a "pit" out of the room by making the box a border around a square or rectangular area that is at floor level. Carpet everything. Many soft pillows and a low coffee table in the center can substitute for the conventional furniture arrangement.

- In a one-room apartment, you can make the bed part of the carpet. Build the bed platform out of plywood in the center or at one end of the room, and cover the whole thing with the same carpet as the rest of the room. The best texture for this type of arrangement is a low-pile plush. Place a foam mattress on top of the carpeted plywood and use whatever you think will make a handsome bedcover. Perhaps you might like to try toweling, fur or just a good-looking sheet.

- Carpeted cubes are a spin-off of the platform. These are handy little items you can make out of extra yardage left over after carpeting a room. In a small parlor, a cube of the same color and texture as the floor is a plus, since it occupies little visual space. You may need an upholsterer's help in getting the corners wrapped neatly—carpet is a lot more difficult to handle than most folks think. A small amount of foam padding on the side to be used for a seat will provide greater comfort, and semiconcealed casters at the base make it easier to move about as you need it.

- Carpet can also be used on walls, although it's hard for one person to handle, and a team of two is usually essential. It also helps if you nail the carpet to the center of the wall in a few places until the outer edges are neat and straight, and then remove the center nails. Carpet on walls softens sound between one room and another, and thus it's a good way to get a quieter room. In addition, it has the visual effect of stretching the space above and beyond the edges of the room. A subtle color like taupe or pearl gray or soft rust is the easiest to work with, as well as being the most practical, although I've seen beautiful walls carpeted in off-white.

- Oriental rugs are very versatile. Bits and pieces can be used for furniture. For example, here's an easy way to make an attractive table or stool using the good part of an old rug (the part that didn't get worn). Cover a large plywood box with the rug and set it on another smaller box for a base. Wrap the carpet all around the upper box, and tack it where the two boxes meet so the tacks won't show. For a super effect, mirror the lower box—this gives the Oriental rug the look of a true flying carpet. With its patterned design and dense weave, the Oriental can absorb a thousand spills, and it also makes a good perching place at a big party if you run out of seats.

- Another way to use leftover Orientals or salvage part of them is to convert them into monster floor pillows which make lovely unusual seats for your room. Let's say your rug is six feet by nine feet, and you can find an unworn piece about three or four feet by six feet. Cut this piece out and fold it in half with the back of the rug on the outside. With a carpet needle and heavy thread, stitch the sides of this remnant together, and then turn it inside out so that now the real carpet surface is on the outside. Fill the pouch with foam pellets and sew the last side closed. Now you have a perfect seat for television-watching or a party.

- Area rugs can make marvelous tapestries. The Scandinavian rya rugs, with their huge single patterns, look more like murals than the real thing, but they are very heavy and therefore need sturdy underpinnings. Sew a thick pocket across the back or use a dozen strong curtain rings to hold the rod that supports the weight of the rug. Brackets bolted into the wall to support the rod are a necessity. Thinner rugs, like those made by Indian or Mexican weavers, are lighter and just as decorative. One of these hanging just over a bed, for example, can take the place of a headboard.

- Maybe you like sheepskin. These luscious, thick rugs are usually one sheep large—not much more than a tiny accent in a big parlor. You can stitch six of them together, making a rug that is roughly nine by nine, and for less than one hundred dollars this assemblage will look like a million. If you can't sew the skins, which requires a special, heavy-duty needle, tape the edges together underneath with carpet tape. Since the skins aren't reversible anyway, the tape won't show.

- One of my favorite tricks is to buy broadloom carpet and have it cut to whatever odd sizes are needed for area rugs in a room. Area rugs usually only come in four-by-six, six-by-nine and nine-by-twelve sizes, but broadloom comes in nine-, twelve- and fifteen-foot-wide widths and any length. This means you can have a rug that is thirteen and a half by fifteen, if that's what will fit your room best, and a matching three-by-fifteen runner for your hall. These can be bound and, if you find the right person to do it, fringed. Or try a border. A wide border of shiny red vinyl on a shaggy white broadloom area rug looks absolutely super.

- If you're starting from scratch and want a combination of wood floor and carpet in your living room, you can combine parquet with carpet easily. First, buy the rug and determine exactly where you want it in the room. Tape around the area where the rug will be and lay the parquet outside this area, leaving a hole for the rug. This may sound like a very cheap trick but it makes no sense at all to waste expensive flooring under carpet.

- The same idea works nicely with ceramic tile, a sensational flooring material. I particularly like the large, eight-inch squares that are now available in all colors, but particularly white. Because it is so easily cleaned, this is one material where you don't have to worry about using white on the floor. Surround the area you want to feature in ceramic with strips of oak in a natural or dark finish, leaving the tile in the conversation area. It makes a lovely focus for the room.

• If you're really down to rock-bottom and cannot afford anything more expensive than vinyl asbestos tile, cheer up. This inexpensive material comes in marvelous solid colors. A combination of beige and white, for example, in a diagonal stripe across a room would make a real conversation stopper, especially if you painted the walls white and upholstered the furniture in inexpensive raw Indian silk in natural beige.

• Sisal is a glorious floor covering. It is available in cheap as well as expensive varieties. You can use the inexpensive kind as wall-to-wall carpeting in your living room. It has a rich, glowing color and a beautiful rough texture that teams up marvelously with white or natural wicker, pale oak, white nubby cotton upholstery and lots of green plants. Sisal is a thin floor covering and wraps easily around plywood. This means that in a small room, you can upholster a large, flat plywood box in the same sisal you are using on the floor and make a coffee-table base. Have a piece of white laminate made to fit the top, or clear glass if you want to keep the look of table and flooring all in one, to stretch the space while providing rich texture.

Lighting, The Indispensable Element

A good interior designer or architect is likely to spend almost as much effort, time and money on lighting a room properly as furnishing it or carpeting it or finding the appropriate window covering. Though it can be expensive, good lighting is always worth it because light has two unique and necessary effects on space—it can fill space and it can enhance it.

The earliest structures of sophisticated man, the temples of Pharaonic Egypt, used light in spectacular ways without the benefit of electricity. In the monolithic hall of the Temple of Karnak, for example, there were giant clerestory windows near the top of the structure, designed for ventilation and to illuminate the incredible painted friezes and bas-reliefs by allowing huge shafts of light to enter. In some of the smaller religious buildings in ancient Egypt, tiny slots were built into two-foot-thick walls to bring a dartlike ray of light into a specific part of the interior, creating dramatic patterns as well as spotlighting the important elements within the temple or tomb.

The Pantheon, a huge Roman temple dedicated to many gods, was built without a single interior column. The giant dome at the top is pierced by a large round opening to the sky. The ceiling is so high that even the heaviest rains are dissipated by the time they reach the floor, and the effect of that huge shaft of light as it enters must have produced a truly religious feeling at the time.

In much the same way, the stained glass used in early Christian churches was designed to produce the same feeling of reverence and awe. In the beguiling church of St. Chapelle in Paris, for example, the Gothic structure is secondary to the glass. Delicate stone fingers arching to the roof hold thousands and thousands of pieces of delectable colored glass, leaded and joined to portray scenes from the Bible as well as to create geometric patterns of all kinds. These glass panels fill every inch of the space between the masonry supports. When sun filters into the church through these amazing panels, it transforms the entire interior into what has often been called a giant lamp of ineffable beauty and inspiration.

In Moslem countries a similar system was used for ceilings in the home. Domed with plaster and stucco, these ceilings were pierced in regular patterns with brilliant blue translucent glass rounds, blue being a sacred color to Moslems. Light entered through these rounds and flooded the interior space with a serene blue glow that is decoration and delight all by itself.

Stained glass is a traditional way of letting light influence space. It has been used in homes for scores of years, each window becoming an elegant lighting fixture for the interior space. Louis Comfort Tiffany designed huge stained-glass screens, meant to stand in front of windows or doorways. In fact, he designed one for the White House which was later sold by a less appreciative president, and Frank Lloyd Wright designed many stained-glass windows for the homes he built.

How Light Fills the Space in Your Room

If it is used creatively, the lighting in any room can be as important an element as large pieces of furniture. Take a large room with very little furniture, a cluster of tall plants, a curved Victorian love seat, a glass coffee table and two rustic director's chairs in natural ash with white canvas seats and backs, all of this arranged around a brown and white cowhide rug. A tall arc lamp illuminates the table top and a brilliant bowl of flowers emerges like a faceted gem. A floodlight in a cylinder on the floor under the plants casts a wide, bright flow of light upward, making the green foliage of the plants as bright as Christmas. An elegant Japanese lantern with a bamboo pole for a stand sways with the leaves of the tallest tree, casting a soft glow on the corner plant cluster, while a very low chromed reading lamp makes the chairs a good place for mending or enjoying a book. The room is sparsely furnished, but the use of a wide variety of related lamps fills the space with diverse kinds of light and shade.

Using Light to Enhance Space

Enhancing space is another property of light, which affects color, texture and finish in many ways. In fact, without light, color and texture do not exist visually.

Light and Color

Color is indeed the quality of the form or shape of any object with respect to the rays of light by which we perceive it. Every one of us has had the experience of trying on a garment in a dimly lighted store dressing room and then taking it to the nearest window to get a better reading on the true color. You can experiment with any color and light by simply exposing a piece of fabric or a paint chip to varying degrees or types of light. No matter what type of light you use, however, the impact of the color is in direct proportion to the amount of light.

A good illustration would be a colored accent wall. In the evening before you illuminate it, a rich blue green wall has about as much zap as a tired pair of overshoes. But if it is illuminated by light reflected from nearby lamps, it begins to take on life. Small pools of its true pigment begin to glow and give dimension to the space. If it is properly and directly lighted by either an overhead track with spots or floods, or a battery of floor-based floods that throw their rays upon the pigment, the blue becomes a true accent in the room.

Light and Texture

In much the same way that pigment is revealed by light, texture does not really exist without it. The richest texture will appear flat and uninteresting in an unlighted space. Once a bit of light filters in, however, a textured carpet becomes a lustrous and rich ornament in the room. Window coverings can be enriched by light as well. A shade or blind of any fabric or texture is, of course, a thing of beauty when daylight enters, but it usually becomes stale and flat when the sun sets. With the proper interior lighting, preferably a ceiling light that washes the wall with light, immensely dramatic effects can be made even with simple and inexpensive window coverings like matchstick blinds. This is because the light brings out the contrast between the high and low surfaces of the texture, dramatizing them far beyond their simple properties.

Light and Finish

Even furniture finishes are subject to change when they are lighted. It is difficult to tell the difference between a matte and glossy finish in an evenly lighted room. Even chrome and glass, those all-time favorites, lose their sparkle in blandly lighted space. Try your hand at spotlighting or pool-lighting with any of the amazingly versatile new portable lights available today. You will find that finishes spring to life, adding visual delight to your room.

Just as light affects color and finish and texture, so, conversely, they affect light. White walls, for example, reflect roughly 75 percent of the available light, whereas a delicious color like dark brown reflects a bare 10 percent. Light color walls, being highly reflective, recede and make a room larger; dark colors advance, making spaces shrink. If you really crave deep dark color on your living room walls, compensate with a white ceiling which will reflect lights, bouncing the rays back into the room, and white woodwork or accents, which will provide reflective contrast to the dark pigment.

Light Levels: Sources and Placement

The level of lighting in your living room is affected by the intensity of the source of light. We all know that a room with a sunny exposure, for example, has a much greater level of light than a room with a northern exposure. Where we often go wrong is equating bulb wattage with foot-candles. Wattage is a measurement not of light but of how much electricity a light is using. A great many folks will increase the wattage of a lamp in an effort to improve the light level in a room, but they really do nothing more than create unpleasant spots of glare. Light levels are measured by lumens or foot-candles. A foot-candle is the intensity of light at any point in your room that is one foot away from a light source equal to one candlepower. This is an antique measuring tool but it is valid because one candle always has the same intensity. The message here is that it is far better to add another source of light to a room than to boost the wattage of a single source and expect it to properly light a remote space.

A good example of this is the traditional light pattern in most living rooms: a pair of lamps on tables on either side of a sofa and another lamp, perhaps for reading, alongside a comfortable chair. What happens to the books in the storage wall? What happens to the plant cluster in the corner? Or the lovely oil painting on the wall opposite the sofa? None of the lamps in the room can adequately illuminate these areas, no matter how much wattage you pump into them. The only way to light them is to add *sources* of light to the room.

A track light with flexible spotlights at various angles will illuminate the books on your storage wall. A separate switch can be installed so that this source of light need not be used except when desired. A floor-based flood lamp lights the plant foliage from beneath; it is plugged into the nearest baseboard receptacle and has its own on-off switch. Another type of light, a recessed wall washer, is focused on the painting and illuminates its extraordinary colors, giving it a depth and power you never noticed before. A wall washer is a flood lamp, mounted near a wall on the surface of the ceiling or recessed below it. The lamp is angled to throw all its illumination on the adjacent wall, and thus it "washes" the wall with its light.

None of these solutions is expensive; with the exception of the installation of the recessed light, it is all work you can do yourself, without an underwriter's certificate. What these new sources of light do is to raise and intensify the light level in your room and give it many new areas of eye interest and visual pleasure, without adding to the wattage.

Light level is measured, finally, in the distance between the light source and the surface it is illuminating. This is plain common sense. It wouldn't make much sense to have a track light six feet from the book titles where the intensity of the foot-candles would be so diminished as to make the light ineffective; or to place a floor flood lamp too far from the plants to illuminate the foliage at the proper angle; or to recess the wall-washer so far from the painting on the wall that not only is its candlepower dissolved but it probably will also blast you in the eye.

There are general rules for the placement of light. Each type of light you use, whether it is a flood, a spot, a recessed wall-washer or even a conventional lamp with an ordinary lampshade, has its own particular spread or intensity arcs radiating from the source and diminishing as the spread moves farther away. The dealers where you buy your lighting fixtures should be able to tell you the proper distance of any light source from the surface you plan to light. Ask them first, and if they sound confused, try your local library.

Different Types of Light Fixtures

There are many different kinds of lighting units on the market today, and using light as a major decorative element in your living room can be as important as color or texture or pattern. I like to think of light in four different descriptions: as utility, as spot, as sparkle, as glow.

Utility Lights

Utility, or task, lights are those we work with—light that is usually directed at the task at hand. To be totally useful, a work lamp should have maximum flexibility. We require a slightly different angle of light for doing needlework than for reading the evening paper, and the light source should be adjustable for both. The current popularity of small, inconspicuous gooseneck lamps (which for so long sold only to physicians) is an indication that people are beginning to realize that lamps are functional sources of light, rather than focal interests in a room.

We have run full cycle and are beginning to utilize the kinds of lamps that provide pure lumens rather than a lot of decorative lamp base. Thus, the doctor's gooseneck lamp has been glorified and redesigned to fit our living rooms. Its finishes are better and more expensive, and its shapes are more elegant, but the principle remains the same. Where work or reading is concerned, a flexible, directable light source serves best.

Clamp lights are another version of the flexible work light. These were originally designed for the architect's or designer's drawing board and are equipped with a springlike contraption that makes it possible to move them in any direction with a fingertip. These entirely satisfying lamps are stylish enough to use in the living room, but if you crave something more elegant you can buy any of the spruced-up versions that combine imagination with function and good light. The clamp lamp often comes with a wall bracket as well, allowing it to take the place of a table lamp and freeing the table surface or, perhaps, doing away with the table altogether.

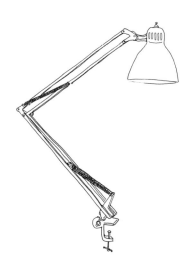

I designed a small living room where there simply was no room for tables on both sides of the sofa. The man who lives in this room likes to read stretched out on the sofa, and to satisfy this entirely normal whim, I hung a wall-mounted lamp at the proper height for sofa reading. The arm of the lamp is long enough for a lateral swing, so that the same lamp provides light if our bachelor friend decides to work or write in the adjacent chair. An ordinary table lamp would not have provided either the direction or the flexibility of this functional lamp.

Spot Lights

Another kind of light that brings variety and versatility to a room is the spot. Spots can be part of a track system; they can be put in an isolated single source hung from or recessed into the ceiling; or they can be attached to a shelf or pole with a swivel-jointed clamp that makes it possible to illuminate a specific area.

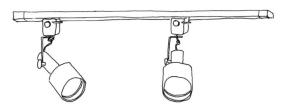

Suppose, for example, you want to light a collection of small black and white drawings hung over a sofa. A track light which can be plugged into a baseboard receptacle would be a simple solution. If the piece you want to feature is a sculpture, however, you might consider a floor-based light. These come in a variety of styles, including several that are simple cylinders of metal, in a brushed chrome, black or white finish, and that have a weighted base that stands firmly on the floor. They are about twelve inches tall, and they accommodate a floodlight bulb of differing wattages, depending on the diameter of the cylinder.

The difference between a spot and a flood is that in a spotlight the form of the fixture or lamp itself directs the flow of light toward an object because it is focused on the object. It is a very specific light and does not have a wide radius of spread. A floodlight bulb provides direction because of its cone shape, its built-in silvered reflector and its lensed surface. These features focus the spread of the light by themselves and so the bulb can be used without any container or lamp at all. Just to make the picture complete, the spotlight lamp very often uses a floodlight bulb for finer definition of the spread radius.

Floor floods are wonderful inventions—they make it possible for anyone to be a lighting genius. If you start out with one, you'll soon want more because they are so versatile. You can use them to light a paint color on a wall because they make the paint glow like a jewel. You can use them to light a corner that is otherwise unused or unfurnished—the light itself furnishes the space. Or you can use them to light plants from beneath, to light a painting or a tapestry or even a piece of lovely framed fabric on the wall. The best part about floor floods is that they are inexpensive, and to make them work all you need to do is plug them into the nearest baseboard receptacle.

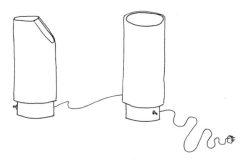

In a small library I designed, I painted the walls a deep rusty apricot, a warm and inviting color. A beautiful Oriental rug in many shades of beiges, browns and apricots is lighted from two table lamps, and two soft modern love seats flank the fireplace, covered in deep brown velour. Behind each love seat and about two feet from the walls I placed a floor-based flood lamp. When I switch these on, the whole room comes to life because all I am doing is lighting color, just the way an electrician lights a stage set. What's more, it is a very restful light because the source is totally hidden behind the sitting furniture, providing a warm rusty environment that makes this the most inviting room in the house.

Light can be spotted from fixed sources as well. By attaching a spot with a swivel base on a fixed rod, like a tension pole, that fits between the ceiling and floor you can light several parts or features of a room. A new twist on this old idea involves big arcs of tempered steel that do not lose their shape, with spots attached, on a swivel for greater flexibility. One famous version of this, made by many manufacturers, is a huge arc based firmly in a block of marble. The steel arc is eight feet in diameter and rises seven feet above the floor, so that anyone can pass under it. From the end of the arc hangs a hemisphere with a lamp and reflector inside it. Although this lamp makes use of a conventional light bulb, it

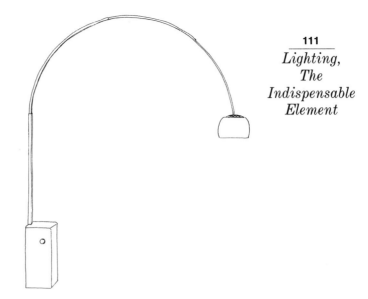

is nonetheless a spot, because it illuminates exactly the area you want, however remote from the source of power.

I tried this spectacular source of light in a tiny living room with four soft swivel chairs around a coffee table in place of the usual sofa, armchair and end table. The only other furnishings in the room were an antique Chippendale desk chair, a lot of plants and an elegant storage wall housing hi-fi, television, a place to work and hundreds of books. The storage wall was lighted with a track light fixed to the ceiling to light the books and small objects of art and a work light fixed to the deeper shelf that formed a writing surface.

I could have looped a lantern from a cord over the coffee table to the ceiling to the nearest wall and then down to a baseboard receptacle, but the very modern chairs and the marble-topped coffee table indicated a more contemporary feeling. I used an arc lamp, with a white marble base of the same type as the coffee table top, just behind one of the four chairs. It arches sumptuously over the chair and then hovers over the table, and provides a source of light just above one's seated sightline. The reflector hides the bulb itself, which lights up the table top with its bowl of bright anemones and changing display of accessories, providing a pleasant glow for conversation and socializing. For reading, two small and inconspicuous gooseneck lamps in the same chrome as the arc lamp flank two of the chairs.

Sparkle Lights

A third type of light is what I call sparkle lights. These are the frills, the icing on the cake of the lighting business. They are lamps or fixtures that are decorative in themselves, not doing any work at all for you, simply looking pretty. Sparkles

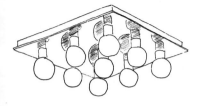

are available in so many different configurations that it is a challenge to list them all.

One I like a lot consists of many small bulbs, their sockets imbedded in a mirrored square that fixes directly to the ceiling. Sparkle can also be a chandelier—an elegant traditional crystal type or the modern version where the glass surrounding the bulbs sparkles rather than the bulbs themselves. Another version of sparkle is tiny Christmas tree lights strung around bare birch branches in a room where you cannot grow plants, or inside a big colored glass jar with a hole drilled in the bottom for the wire. Sparkle can also be lamps that are programmed to go on and off just for fun. These can be amusing and attractive but not as a steady diet. In general, sparkle lights are a tremendous visual boost to a long and boring hall which one just passes through rather than to a living room which is used intensively and steadily.

Glow Lights

A final type of light is the glow light. These have become increasingly popular in the last ten years and come in many forms. Ceiling or wall fixtures that glow include the familiar translucent globes or cylinders or squares. These diffuse the light of the electric bulb within, creating a pleasant glow that also illuminates space. The same shapes are available as table or floor lamps on thin stems, and many other versions have also been developed. Some glow lamps have glass or metal shades that look like the spreading petals of a flower; others are just Japanese lanterns that have been attached to bamboo rods, or equipped with little legs to stand on their own, and stretched and changed into different shapes. The same idea has been used with fabric attached to a wire frame rather than to the rice paper of the traditional Japanese lantern.

More modern forms of glow lights are the chromed steel columns equipped with globes which come in many different shapes and sizes. One of the nicest glow lights I've used is a small, eight-inch-square cube of translucent glass, lighted from within. This little light makes a marvelous pedestal for any small piece of sculpture, lighting it gently from below. Tiffany, or Tiffany-type, lamps are a fine example of glow. The source of the light is invisible, but it illuminates the huge variety of colored glass in these marvelous creations. Just turning one on makes me feel cheerful.

Even furniture has been converted into glow lights. There are cubes with translucent plexiglas or glass tops that diffuse light from a bulb within—a marvelous way to light a dull corner. The latest invention, a large spheroid electric bulb which comes coated, clear or colored, is like a lamp all by itself. By setting these bulbs into a porcelain socket in the ceiling or into a series of sockets on a lighting strip attached to ceiling or wall, you can create inexpensive and attractive glow lighting where you want it.

You may think that many of these sources of light sound too modern for your living room. I believe we are too sophisticated today to be overly conformist in lighting styles. Mixing modern lighting fixtures or lamps with more traditional styles is something that is not only sensible, it is also preferable because a great many modern lamps are unobtrusive while they are doing their job.

In a living room I worked on, for example, there were two sets of crystal wall sconces, one set at the door and the other over the mantel, which itself is a lovely marble antique piece. On a music cabinet that holds stereo equipment and records I used a lovely Tiffany lamp in glowing colors of green; a gorgeous Lucite sculpture in greens and yellows is lighted with an almost invisible floor floodlight; a very modern pair of chrome gooseneck lamps make task lights for the sofa; and a lamp made of a pale blue antique ginger jar of translucent glass with a white pleated paper shade stands on a table next to the armchair. A wild combination of styles, to be sure, but somehow they all hold together because they are in scale with the space and the furnishings, which are about 75 percent traditional and the balance contemporary.

Planning the Lighting in Your Living Room

Lighting, like furniture, must be planned. Not surprisingly, many of the same guidelines that apply to color and furniture also apply to a lighting plan. Scale, balance and unity are as important in lighting space as they are in the plan of furniture or in the application of color in the same space.

Lighting and Scale

Scale in lighting implies that the light sources in the room relate not only to the space but also to the furnishings and colors of the room. Obviously, the light must be in scale with the space in order for it to do its job. It would be as silly to use a few scattered lamps with a low lumen count in a large room as it would be to use a huge floodlight in a tiny room. This is just plain common sense. Your eye will tell you immediately if there is sufficient light in any room simply by how difficult or easy it is to perceive details of form and color. A good guideline is that there should be at least four sources of light in any living room, no matter the size. In large rooms there should be more foot-candles as well as more light sources. Lighting depends on surrounding colors and textures, on how far or near the source of the light is to the object it illuminates and on the foot-candle power. Thus it is only fair to say that light must be scaled sensibly to space.

Light can be scaled more readily to colors than to space. In a room with dark walls the pigment absorbs the light, and more foot-candles will be necessary. If walls and ceilings are white or very light colors that reflect light, fewer

foot-candles can be used. The type of fixture or lamp must also be scaled to the color. Floodlights that illuminate dark or rich colors on walls, floors or in fabrics can be used in track lighting, or in floor-based lamps. Floodlights can also be mounted so that they are flush with the surface of the wall or ceiling, or they can be recessed below the surface. Glow lights work well in dark rooms, as well. In a room with white walls and light colors in general, more of the small task and sparkle lamps and fixtures can be used, since overall illumination is not as crucial.

The scale of any lamp or fixture must also relate to the surrounding or supporting furniture. A table lamp must not be larger than the table that supports it, although we have all seen lamps that are certainly taller and more monstrous than the tables on which they sit. More important, however, is that the scale of the cumulative total of light in the room should not overwhelm the furniture. A good example of this would be the small room with a large lamp on every table in the room, each lamp holding a 200 watt bulb. Of course, a rheostat or dimmer can help scale down the effect of too much light, and these come in many guises. You can attach a dimmer to a ceiling light simply by rewiring the switch to accommodate the rheostat. For table lamps, there are portable dimmers that look like oversize matchboxes and sit on the table near the lamp. Some lamps are even made with built-in dimmers.

Lighting and Balance

Planning with light also involves balance. Lamps and fixtures must have enough variety to balance one another. A room full of pharmacist's lamps would look plain silly; so would a room full of sparkle lights, or a room full of nothing but glow lights, or a center ceiling light with a 200 watt bulb. The trick is to plan each light to fit the needs of the space, while striving to preserve a balance of style and size. In general, a good guideline to follow is that you should not use more than two of any type, unless you are striving for a very special effect. I designed a studio living room, for example, where two sofa beds were connected at right angles with a corner table. On this table sprouted eight gooseneck lamps fastened to the plywood top of the table with cleats. These lamps were made from pieces of flexible tubing cut to three different lengths for the goosenecks themselves, eight small reflectors, switches, sockets, wire and bulbs. This cluster of flexible lights provided task lights, sparkle and spots for anyone or anything in the vicinity of the seating area. All the remaining light in the room was provided by light tracks on two opposite walls. It was definitely a case of special effects! (See page 116).

A good balance of light in a living room normally involves a wider variety of light. I worked on a room that had a northern exposure and desperately needed as much light as I could provide. Two different table lamps with similar translucent linen shades flank the sofa on unmatched tables; a Tiffany student lamp lights the antique secretary opposite the sofa on one side of the fireplace; a

brass floor lamp with a brass reflector on a swivel provides a reading light for the comfortable leather chair and ottoman; a floor spot lights the painting on the wall between the windows; and two surface-mounted wall-washers (see page 107) light the front of the secretary and the shelves on the other side of the fireplace. On one of these shelves stands a beautiful stained-glass sculpture with its own built-in light, a small showcase bulb whose light is reflected back onto the white wall behind the sculpture, creating a multicolored glow for the room. In this plan the light sources balance each other, antique with modern, as in the furnishings. Glow, task and spot lights all work together (page 118).

Different kinds of lights make a room as interesting as different colors or paintings or fabrics or styles. But remember that too much variety can be worse that none at all. You don't want your room to look like a lamp store. A good procedure is not to buy all your lamps at the same time. Add them in easy stages—perhaps a pair first, then a single, later a spot or flood and last of all the decorative glow or sparkle lamps, almost like accessories, for added verve and pizazz.

Lighting and Unity

When your lamps and fixtures are in scale with the space and the furnishings, and your lighting scheme is balanced, you can achieve a kind of lighting karma, or unity, within a room. The choice of any lamp must be made with care, taking into account the size, style and shape of the space it must illuminate. Dimmers help your room adjust to daily and seasonal changes of daylight as well as helping to balance your lighting plan. But the properly lighted room will have more than just a pleasant or interesting collection of different lamps and fixtures; their combined illumination will produce the unity your room needs.

A BAKER'S DOZEN TRICKS WITH LIGHTS

• With a bit of ingenuity and a few basic materials you can make a reasonable facsimile of the popular clamp light—the kind you can attach to a shelf to light a work surface below or books or art objects above. At a photography store, buy a clamp and reflector shade, the kind made for a flash bulb attachment. From your local hardware store, buy a socket with a switch in it, enough cord to get from the shelf to the nearest receptacle and a plug. For approximately seven dollars and about half an hour of your time, you're in business.

• If you don't like the ceiling light your landlord gave you, you can replace it yourself—carefully—or ask your local electrician to do it. Buy the simplest possible socket and base of spun or polished aluminum. The base should be wide enough to cover the existing opening in the ceiling. Buy a circle of mirror sixteen inches in diameter, and have your mirror dealer cut a hole in the center

which is a half-inch or so smaller than the outer diameter of the new fixture base. Also have your mirror dealer polish the outer edges of the circle. The fixture will hold the mirror in place on the ceiling. Use a globelight, one of those elegant spheroid electric bulbs, in a clear finish to add sparkle to this elegant new fixture.

- Globelights can also be used as pendant ceiling lights. Buy thick vinylized wire, white porcelain sockets and white cord switches. String up wire and sockets in a grouping of three or four different lengths, or all the same if you prefer. Hang these from white hooks placed so that the bulbs are at least six or eight inches apart, and then run the rest of the cord in a cluster to the nearest baseboard receptacle. Loop the strands of wire in one bunch as it reaches the ceiling. This is a simple version of glow lighting. For the best effect use the translucent rather than the clear globelights.

- White porcelain sockets are versatile. Attach them to walls on white, glossy self-stick paper cut out in circles of different diameters. Place these in a cloud on the wall, then fasten the socket in the center of each, trailing the white cord off to a baseboard receptacle. Use a small translucent bulb in each socket. On a navy blue wall these circles look like so many moons. A star pattern works well, too.

- There are certain types of light bulb sockets which don't have to be mounted in a lamp, and you can use them to create marvelous light sculptures. Check your local hardware store for one particular variety which has three distinct parts: a plug end which will fit into any wall receptacle, a socket which will hold a light bulb and a receptacle which will receive any standard two-pronged plug. You can string these socket-plugs together, since each one has a light bulb of its own, and build many unusual lighted shapes. Try a tall, branching column to give the effect of a lighted tree in your living room.

- Sometimes you may have an unwanted ceiling outlet in the middle of the living room. Here is a good way to make use of power from this awkwardly placed outlet, without going to the expense of plastering over it or buying a costly fixture to hang from it. Cover the outlet with a mounting canopy, which is available at most hardware stores. Mounting canopies are usually round with a hole in the middle for an electrical wire to go through, and they are made of metal or porcelain. These canopies are designed specifically for the purpose of covering over the gaping hole left in the ceiling when an electrical outlet is made. You can paint your canopy any color which fits your scheme, and drop a long, thick vinyl wire with a bulb and socket at the end through the canopy. Then cover the bulb with a shade of any kind—a Japanese lantern, a bowl, anything which suits your taste. Hang this over a low spacious coffee table with chairs or sofas or settees placed around in a large square, allowing the furniture as well as the new fixture to float in space.

- Fluorescent tubes can provide interesting lighting effects as well. They come in an eight-foot-long variety which can be mounted vertically on the wall from ceiling to floor, providing a subtle and inexpensive illumination. Or use them just above the baseboard on a single long wall in your living room. They are especially effective if you have dark floors. Fluorescent tubes are particularly attractive if mounted on both walls of an uninteresting corridor, for example.

- Some cheapies come already assembled. My favorite is the work light used by construction workers. This lamp comes with a convenient hook at the top, a long cord that can reach from one end of the room to another and a switch on the socket. It can be hooked up wherever you need an occasional light. A cluster of three or four is particularly effective, especially if you find the kind that are made with an orange or yellow vinyl safety cord, socket and plug and a polished chrome hood and wire mask.

- You can make a lamp that looks like a piece of sculptured snow by pasting together a set of those marvelous polystyrene crating materials, the kind television sets and other valuables come wrapped in. Use a white glue to hold the polystyrene forms together. A piece of plywood at the base holds the socket, and an ordinary 60 or 100 watt bulb is ample to make this glow lamp work.

- Changing the color of the bulbs in your glow lamps is fun. Bulbs come in at least four colors—blue, red, green and yellow. You can give your room a whole new look by simply putting a different color bulb in a lamp that is a square or sphere of translucent glass or plastic.

- If you want a really inexpensive lamp, try a perforated paper bag as a shade. White paper gives the most light, but the ordinary brown paper bag has a more natural look. Suspend the bulb on a cord over a medium-sized table. Cut many random small holes in the paper bag with your paper punch and slit open the closed end. Place the bag over the bulb, with the slit end up, and gather the paper around the cord well above the socket with a strong rubber band. The bulb itself should hang at the center of the bag. The paper should be strong and stiff enough so that the bag will remain open. You can reinforce the bottom edge with a band of cardboard to keep the bag open. Make sure to use a small bulb within a fairly large bag so that the flammable paper shade isn't ignited by the hot bulb.

- Leftover Christmas tree lights are very inexpensive after the holidays and make marvelous light murals. Buy three or four strings of these (on white cord if possible) and substitute clear miniature bulbs for the colored ones. Choose a spot on a plain wall where a light mural will work, and lightly draw the pattern you want in chalk on the wall. Then staple the light cords to the wall with a staple gun so that the part with the plug ends up near a floor receptacle. I've made wild and intricate abstractions with these light paintings, and they are effective on either a dark or light wall.

- A general tip for living room lights is not to fix them permanently so that they are immovable. Changing the lighting is a very effective and simple way to change the personality of a room. Moving a glow light to another table can give an entire area a new look; a floor-based floodlight in a new corner can illuminate a completely different group of furniture or accessories; and a sparkle light in a different place is a totally new accent in itself. Such changes provide a cheap way to keep your decorating fresh and alive for you and your friends.

Accessories The Finishing Touch

We have spent a lot of time going over the fundamentals of designing your living room. Now we are going to talk about the embellishments—the extras that are called accessories. The manufacture of accessories has grown into a huge business. We are learning that accessories are more than an ashtray or a vase to hold flowers, but are rather another form of decorative art, and there is no end to the variety and richness of this art today.

I'm sure you all have the same complaint that I've heard from so many people, which is simply that they can't see the forest for the trees. Even the smallest store is loaded with many ideas for accessories, and the displays and model rooms are so enticing that shopping for decorative art today can be a mind-blowing experience. In this chapter we're going to explore the many different types of accessories and what they can do for your living room. Then we will look at the mechanics—how to select and display these to their best advantage and your greatest visual pleasure.

All the while you are doing this you are asking, isn't it enough to furnish my living room in the latest style? Furnishings are not enough; a good example is the contemporary hotel room. Usually well designed, it may have a picture or two on the wall, but beyond that it is pretty bare of personality. Since it accommodates such a huge variety of guests and tastes, it is more like an unwritten book or an empty vase, just waiting for the right words or flowers to fill the void. Furnishings fill a space; accessories finish it.

This finishing process, so important to the look of the room, is important for another reason. Accessories, whether an important painting or the tiniest box or basket, are a key to your personality. If you are the kind of person who only reproduces the accessories your friends have, your room will look like theirs, not yours. If, on the other hand, you are individualistic and interested enough to strike out on your own and to plan your accessories just the way you have planned your furnishings, you will have a room that is a personal extension of this interest and individualism.

Types of Accessories

Let's look at the different kinds of accessories that finish a room. They can be roughly divided into two categories: the functional and the decorative.

Functional

The functional include those pieces that do a job for you, from ashtrays to candlesticks, vases, boxes, baskets and pillows. Each of these is manufactured today in tremendous profusion and in a galaxy of colors, styles, shapes and sizes. Thus it is possible to feature or accent one or more as the principal accessory in your room, as well as to use it for a practical purpose. I designed a room, for example, where a collection of antique crystal candlesticks dominated a coffee table. None of them matched, but they worked together because they were all crystal and all served the same function.

Decorative

The other category is the decorative accessory, also a familiar part of every living room. This category would include art of all kinds, from paintings to prints to posters to photographs. It would include the whole gamut of sculpture, from the traditional formal sculpture carved of marble or cast in bronze, to the popular wire sculptures of today, to a huge shell on a Lucite pedestal. I've even placed a small, sleek and well-designed black-and-white television set on a white lacquered pedestal and treated it like a piece of beautiful sculpture.

Collections

Collections really fit into the decorative category, though they may also be useful objects that are being used as decoration. I've seen a whole wall decorated with porcelain lids from china casseroles, pot-de-creme cups, paté molds, soup tureens and just about anything that has a decorative cover. Not only was this a unique and decorative wall, it also told a lot about the owner, who was a gourmet cook and spent a great deal of time browsing through antique shops for old pieces. The lids themselves were often the leftovers from previous whole sets, a good way to use the top when the bottom breaks.

A collection could also consist of baskets or boxes or a whole cluster of small framed prints, etchings or drawings. I worked on a living room for a family with two gifted artist daughters whose childhood work was so good that it had to be displayed in the living room. I covered one small wall with homosote (an inexpensive building material that comes in four-by-eight-foot sheets) and papered this with the same textured grass-cloth wall covering that I used in the rest of the room. The children's work, constantly changing and becoming more sophisticated, was tacked to the wall in carefully thought-out arrangements and could easily be taken down for replacement or improvement without leaving unsightly holes. Another simple system for a collection that changes, like photographs, is to use instant frames, those inexpensive plexiglas boxes, where the back comes out in a second and the "art" can be replaced at the drop of a paintbrush or camera.

Plants and Flowers

Then there is another subcategory of accessories that is both functional and decorative—plants and flowers. A good case could be made that plants are useful because they not only supply a great deal of nitrogen and oxygen to an indoor atmosphere, but they also have therapeutic value to the gardener. As a plant lover myself, I cannot think of a better way to unwind than to spend an hour repotting a fast-growing plant or spraying or watering my plant collection.

Mirrors

Mirrors are also a subcategory of accessories that is both functional and decorative. In a very narrow, long living room, with three small windows at the far end, I installed floor-to-ceiling mirrors from the windows along the wall to a distance of four feet back. I then mirrored the ceiling between the mirrored wall areas as well, using mirrored squares with self-adhesive backing. The space in front of these mirrors was filled with a bentwood rocker. This space was thus converted into a greenhouse by reflecting the windows and the outdoor and indoor plants, and the space was broadened visually.

Planning the Accessories in Your Living Room

In planning to use accessories in your living room, the same guidelines apply for the choice, selection and placement of these delightful goodies as for furniture, color and lighting. Scale, balance, color and style are important factors in choosing and displaying anything from a pillow to a painting. But don't be dogmatic about any of these; it's easier to use an accessory you already own in a spot where you think it will work than to worry too much about formal guidance. It is helpful, however, to use these guidelines before purchasing any costly items.

Accessories and Scale

Start with scale. The following example of bad accessory planning should be very instructive. A painting that is larger than the sofa or table under it is a disaster because it makes the sofa or table less important in the room and also gives one a top-heavy feeling that is downright uncomfortable. Within a group of accessories, scale is equally important. In a collection of boxes, for example, it doesn't matter whether they are tin, brass, straw or lacquer because if one is too large for the others it just won't fit. This sore-thumb concept is easy to remember; in a collection, try to keep like things of similar sizes, whereas unlike objects can be vastly different in scale.

Accessories and Balance

All this relates to balance as well. In a room I designed there is a table-top grouping of very different items. These include an interesting mask from New Guinea made of a turtle shell originally covered over with mud and later painted in a primitive pattern of black, brown, white and rust. The whole thing is mounted on a block of clear Lucite. With this mask is a low, flat African basket in natural straw with two handles, a heart-shaped French Limoges box in the same bright rust color as the mask, a modern black cigarette lighter and two identically shaped ashtrays in different shades of rust enamel. All this is set on a black lacquer Chinese table in front of a sofa. Though the mask is the largest of the accessories, the rust color is balanced by the intense concentration of the same color in the small Limoges box and in the identical ashtrays.

Balance can be illustrated in a different way. You have a collection of handsome prints, but there is one that is much larger than the others. Rather

than placing this in the center surrounded by prints in smaller frames, which gives the feeling of dropping off into space on either side, place it at one end of the collection. This allows the other, subordinate works to fill the space. Then balance the big print with a tall plant on a table at the far end or with a pair of tall candlesticks.

Accessories and Color

Accessories must be planned according to color as well. If you have a collection of interesting objects, it makes more sense to group them by colors, even if doing this breaks up other groups. Imagine a room where there is a basic color scheme of deep green and white. A group of handsome amethyst minerals on small stands would look smashing on a white end table, while a collection of white ironstone candlesticks would provide a crisp accent on the glass top of the coffee table. But mixing these two groups, with their distinctive color characteristics, would be a disaster!

Color is exploitable. Suppose you want a collection, but you don't have the money or the experience, as yet, to buy valuable paintings or drawings. You can frame a half-dozen black and white prints very inexpensively by matting them all with the same color—a clear bright yellow for example—in simple frames with thin chrome edges. This creates a unified family of prints out of a lot of diversity. Color can be a unifying element in developing a collection of color prints as well. Just be sure that your choices have one key color in common and they will all work together, even if they are works of many different artists and many different sizes and shapes.

Accessories and Style

Choosing accessories according to style is another way to plan. The following sections will help to illustrate this concept through examples of specific rooms I have designed in a variety of styles.

Early American

If you have an Early American living room, it would be downright silly to buy a group of plexiglas sculptures or a huge modern abstract painting. This doesn't mean that everything in your room has to be from the same period, but it must look appropriate to the space. In your living room, with its Early American furniture, you might have a beautiful pinewood mantel over the fireplace at perfect eye level for a collection of turned wood candlesticks of different shapes. Against the white walls, these become a focal point in the room. Nothing more is needed at the fireplace except perhaps a pair of decorative and useful black iron tongs for handling logs and a huge wicker laundry basket, stained dark brown, to hold the logs. Behind the Chippendale camel-back settee, at a right angle to the fireplace, is a smashing collection of brass pots and pitchers used interchangeably for plants, flowers and coffee, as necessary. On the coffee table, which is basically an overscaled butler's tray, between the settee and two facing chairs of simple, contemporary style is a handsome pewter set of small bowls used for nuts or candies or just as ashtrays.

All these accessories are appropriate to the style of the room, yet they are not authentic in the true sense of the word. Some of the candlesticks came from England from a much earlier period than American colonial, and two of them were made by an imaginative craftsman in California and are not Early American at all. Yet all the candlesticks were made with the same kind of wood-turning device and therefore fit into the group. The brass pieces came from Turkey, Israel, Egypt and India. The pewter bowls are faithful reproductions of Early American bowls, and one of them is a very old piece from France. But all these interesting shapes fit the room and group happily together.

Victorian

Like other styles, a Victorian room can be accessorized with a diversity of objects both functional and decorative. Such a room can be a splendid background for a large, modern canvas or a collection of smaller works, provided they are related in color.

In a lovely Victorian house I worked on, I used a fabulous tufted sofa of the period, covered in a modern white velour. Over the elaborately carved marble mantle I hung a truly decorative, huge antique mirror with a gilded frame. Two small tufted side chairs of the period in the same white were placed opposite the sofa, and between these and the sofa there was a glorious Japanese black lacquer table. On this table I arranged a collection of many heavy antique brass keys and a brilliant rose red bowl. Two big ferns stood on clear plexi pedestals on one side of the sofa; on the other side was a simple modern brass lamp. The walls are a deep green paint, with crisp white woodwork and white mini-slat Venetian blinds. On the polished hardwood floor is a glorious kilim rug with a black background and cabbage roses in greens and reds, looking for all the world like a real Aubusson, while the fireplace contains brass andirons and a very modern set of brass firetools.

The tall plexi pedestals look right because they are the proper scale for the high-backed, full-blown Victorian style; the gilded frame of the mirror makes the modern brass lamp appropriate, as well as the contemporary firetools. The keys, some older than Queen Victoria and some a good deal younger, make an interesting and decorative collection and they are balanced by the modern ceramic red bowl, often filled with a pot of ivy or a big bunch of green grapes.

French

Even a French parlor can use a variety of accessories if you follow the guidelines of scale, balance and color. I worked on a room with walls painted in the palest tint of pink; the furniture was a collection itself. A French sofa and two open-arm occasional chairs with pale fruitwood frames were covered in deep gray moiré; an elegant bergère (a larger, upholstered armchair) was covered in off-white silk. These pieces surrounded a modern coffee table with a pinkish marble top on a chrome frame. I chose a pale gray plush wall-to-wall carpet to make this small room seem more expansive. The windows were covered simply with fruitwood shutters. All the pattern in the room was in the accessories, because on the walls, wherever there was an inch, was a splendid collection of very modern, abstract small paintings in singles, in doubles and in clusters. They were all by different artists but they were framed in plain thin chrome frames. This and their small size helped make them work together, so they acted almost like wallpaper in this otherwise simple room.

Between the two windows I placed a fruitwood pedestal, to match the shutters, on which was a superb chrome sculpture—almost a sphere, balanced on a thin rod, making it seem to float in space. A smaller version of the piece by the same sculptor stands on a smaller fruitwood cube on the coffee table. On this same table stands a cut crystal bowl containing a bunch of bright flowers in colors that come from the paintings. The bowl is flanked by a cut crystal decanter and two elegant tall-stemmed sherry glasses on a plexi tray with chrome handles. For this formal room, two fig trees (*Ficus exotica,* a fruitless fig tree) were cut and pruned to look like huge lollipop trees. They stand in big wicker baskets which I sprayed with glossy white paint. Smaller, flowering plants cluster at the baskets' bases, so that a seasonal change of plants makes an instant color change in the room.

Contemporary

Contemporary rooms make marvelous backgrounds for all kinds of accessories, modern, antique or just "found junk." Somehow the simple squared shapes of modern furniture and the big expanses of white or bright colors make these rooms a comfortable place for anything from a huge modern abstract canvas to a delicate Japanese carved stone Buddha. I designed a contemporary country room for a couple who love to collect things on their many trips to far away places. The modern furniture was elegant and understated. A pale natural leather modular seating group against white textured walls made a wide U-shape around two travertine marble cubes that took the place of a coffee table. Behind one of the modular seats is a low Parsons table in white lacquer, and in a corner at the window is a series of white lacquer pedestals of different heights and thicknesses. The pedestals hold two beautiful African carved wood statues—their very primitive features a counterpoint to the plain whiteness of their stands—and two large grape ivy plants in natural wicker baskets from Nigeria with a black pattern woven through. These pedestals are easy to make yourself from plywood, if you are handy.

The windows are covered with a combination of hinged mirrored panels and natural matchstick bamboo shades. The mirrors reflect the plants and sculpture as well as acting as "draperies." On one of the marble cubes are three beautiful black lacquer boxes from Japan and a modern crystal ashtray from Sweden. On the other table is a Swedish crystal budvase which holds a flamboyant red rose, or a fresh anemone or a tulip or whatever else is in season, and a black lacquer Japanese bowl for nuts or candies. On the table behind the sofa is a glass glow lamp in a large spherical shape, three smaller pre-Columbian primitive sculptures on small white pedestals, a round wooden butter press and a superb antique wooden model of a Japanese country house, complete with sliding shoji doors. All these accessories provide a fascinating balance for the large modern abstract painting over the sofa, in hues of browns and beiges on a white background.

More about Collections

Using collections as accessories is like painting a big canvas and then adding tiny dabs of exciting color or texture to the background. Nothing has to be exactly the same style, color or size as anything else in the collection as long as the items you select and display are related in one of these ways. The same is true of the collection wall. Many people collect lots of tiny paintings or works of art, each one too small to hang by itself. But if you cluster them over a sofa or a console or credenza, they can work together to substitute for the big painting or print you can't afford this year. But to make them work they must be chosen with care and assembled and hung with a definite shape in mind.

I worked on a collection for a couple who had gathered some interesting old baskets, a Shaker pitchfork, four eighteenth-century Greek wood shuttles (the long wand used to carry the yarn through the warp in weaving) and a set of six sepia prints of heads of children, reproductions from a museum collection. I framed the prints with a thin white frame and a light brown mat, similar to the color of the shuttles, the baskets and the pitchfork. Then I hung the whole collection, using the larger pieces as ballasts and the smaller to fill the spaces in between, over a pair of low oak cubes which are used as extra tables for guests. With a cluster of plants nearby and a track light overhead, this simple collection of inexpensive objects and art looks like an arrangement in a museum gallery.

I used the shape of a horizontal rectangle as the outer edge for this collection, but there can be many variations on this theme. You can use a vertical rectangle if you want to stretch the height of a low ceiling, and you can balance this shape with a tall plant or lamp at the other end of the room. Remember that the eye travels fast and will register the balance in a room in a split second. You can use a round outer shape, but this would depend a great deal on the items you were arranging. Square prints, for example, would be difficult to arrange in a big circle. But if you had your children's photos from over the years put in round or oval gold frames, you could happily use a circle as the outer shape. Perhaps this big circle would go well over a high white Parsons table with a spotlight (hidden by a few flowering plants) to focus on the photos. This can be a marvelous way to make family pictures part of your decorating scheme.

Squares, diamonds—any shape—can work as the outer shape of your collection, depending on the items you are displaying and their shapes and sizes. You don't need a professional to help you. To make your collection work in the space and shape you have decided on, measure the outer edges of the area on the wall where the collection will go. Then just lay the whole thing out on the floor, in exactly the relationship each piece will be to the others on the wall. Make sure that the outer edges of the pieces conform to the overall dimensions you have measured. From there it is easy to decide exactly where the nails or picture hooks should go on the wall without making a lot of unnecessary holes.

Do-It-Yourself Accessories

Do-it-yourself accessories are also on the upswing. Pillows made of tie-dyed fabric, needlepoint, patchwork and crewel, boxes covered with shells you've collected, boxes covered with paper cutouts and shellacked, small hooked accent rugs, your own photos or paintings or collages and many more make lovely personalized touches for your living room. There is nothing more satisfying than making something beautiful for your home, and you don't have to be an artist or sculptor to be creative.

In a living room I designed in a city apartment, I used a brown, black and white color scheme. The walls were brown and on the wood floor in front of the sofa and chairs, I used a zebra rug. Fortunately, the world's zebra population is alive and well, but if you don't like animal skins you could use a brown, black and white area rug in wool or acrylic yarns for much the same effect. The sofa is covered in white cotton and the two modern chairs at right angles to it are made of chrome and tufted natural leather. For two mobile ottomans on the other side of the sofa, I designed a needlework pattern in a zebralike design, with zebra colors. The pattern called for rug canvas and thick yarn so that the work would go fast. The owner did the work (it only took a few weeks), and we then had a professional upholster the ottomans with the finished canvas. They look sumptuous and original—there's nothing else around quite like them. A mirrored cube for the coffee table reflects the zebra pattern on the floor and in the needlepoint on the ottomans.

For another needlepoint enthusiast whose yard boasted a fantastic tulip poplar tree, I designed three pillows in a finer canvas, using the delicate tulip tree flowers as the motif. The room was designed in a blend of the flower colors—pale yellows, apricots, off-whites and fresh greens—and the handmade pillows provided the perfect accent.

Changing Accessories

Accessories are the most versatile part of home furnishings because they are easy to change or move. One of the nicest kinds of changes is the seasonal switch. Actually, you don't have to move everything—just switch pillows, plants, flowers and accent accessories.

I worked on a room for a woman who loved to change the look from winter to summer without working too hard at it. For a year-round color I used white

vinyl flooring and white painted walls for the greatest flexibility. In the winter, a small, thick brown patterned rug in a tiny herringbone design is placed in front of the seating group, which is basically a white flare-armed sofa, a cane chair with a soft cushion in the same brown as the rug and two simple armless lounge chairs covered in brown velour. From its place over the sofa, a large abstract painting in shades of brown, amber and rust gives an instant seasonal feeling of fall and winter. Four small bold abstract prints in black, brown and white, framed in chrome, are grouped on the wall behind the chairs. The pillows are different patterns of brown and white batik, while russet chrysanthemums cluster in a square glass bowl on the delicate walnut antique desk near the sofa. A silver cigarette box, a pair of cut crystal candlesticks and a brown and white Japanese ceramic bowl are arranged on the plexiglas coffee table.

In the spring, a new look is created by changing the painting to one in which pale lavender, pale lemon yellow and pale taupe are painted on a white background. The winter painting is wrapped in vinyl sheeting and stored in the coat closet, flat against the wall, with a piece of plywood separating it from the coats. The pillows are exchanged for silk and cotton pillows in lavender and lemon. A straw rug in the taupe of the painting replaces the dark brown winter version; the brown chairs are slipcovered in zippered white cotton duck; and the cane chair loses its brown seat cushion for the duration. The four bold prints are switched to four white-on-white ones by simply removing the art from the take-apart frames and refastening them over new summer prints. Lavender bachelor's buttons or the palest yellow zinnias fill the vase all summer. A large schefflera tree is moved further away from the very sunny window and small cane plants in wicker baskets take their place on the coffee table. It's not much of a switch, but it changes the whole look of the room from the deep rich browns and russets of winter to the light white and pale flower colors of summer—a welcome change for little effort.

Plants As Accessories

Plants are a large part of today's accessorizing. Not too many years ago, some folks thought it was too difficult to grow green plants and used plastic ones instead. In fact, even the plant or florist shops sold plastic. All that is changed today. Whether it is the new interest in conservation and appreciation of nature, or the fact that people have more education in horticulture, there's just no doubt that plants are in. A room without plants today is rare. Some rooms are even overplanted, just as they can be overaccessorized or overfurnished or overcolored.

The important thing to remember in accessorizing with plants is their place. No matter how much you fertilize, spray and talk to a plant, if the place isn't right it won't live there for long. I've always maintained that you can tell in a

week's time whether the location is appropriate, just by the look of the plant. Its leaves should be glossy, new growth should be evident and the whole plant should look sprightly and happy. Check with your plant book or florist before you buy that *Ficus benjamina* for the corner, because if the corner doesn't get a lot of bright sunlight, that big plant is going to drop its leaves and become a bad investment.

On the other hand, a plant in a good location goes on thriving for years, even if you don't fertilize, spray or say a blessed word to it. I have a Boston fern that now has a wingspread of five feet; it has been repotted three times and has lived in three different homes—but always in a window facing east.

Small table-top plants, like any accessory, can and should be moved to take advantage of changing light, or be switched with plants at the window. Plants look their best when clustered by species, so don't try to mix a lot of different types.

No matter what your choice in accessories, there are two basic looks for a room—restrained elegance and controlled clutter. The first is simple; a few very good things are selected and displayed prominently. The other look is controlled clutter; lots of goodies are displayed artfully and carefully, with a specific place for each object. Either of these looks can adapt to any style room or any type of accessory, and the best way to find out which you like best is to experiment. Accessories are so easy to move that you can shift them around until you achieve just the right finishing touch that makes your room a happy statement of your own lifestyle.

A BAKER'S DOZEN TRICKS WITH ACCESSORIES

- Write for outdoor posters from companies like Volkswagen and Seven Up. These ads are like wallpaper, but they come in large sections instead of rolls. They can be put up with wallpaper paste to cover a wall or most of it. Most manufacturers will gladly sell this super-art at cost plus postage—it's a bargain.

- Beautiful fall leaves from maples, sycamores, oaks or a handy chestnut tree provide instant art for your living room. Arrange them in neat rows in a plexiglas instant frame, where all you have to do is pull out the back to change the art. The leaves will dry to a beautiful rich tawny beige, a handsome addition to a white wall. A series of these framed leaves could make a fascinating collection wall in a room where naturals prevail.

- A quilt makes a beautiful large work of art. You don't have to pay an arm and a leg for an antique quilt, although these are undoubtedly the most beautiful. There are many modern quilts that make fabulous wall hangings, or if you're being economical, try the baby department in your local store for a smaller version that costs a lot less. Sew a narrow muslin pocket on the back of the quilt at one end and run a curtain rod through this for hanging. But be sure the colors work with your room, or it will just look like you're hanging out the laundry.

- A collection of hats can make a marvelous wall decoration. Buy a dozen of the inexpensive straw variety stocked by stores in early summer. There is usually a representative sampling from such exotic places as Italy, Hong Kong, the Philippines and Guatemala. When they are placed in an enormous rectangle or square arrangement, the similar shapes and natural fibers can make you look like a world traveler as well as provide a wall with handsome texture for your room. A set of hats on an antique floor hatrack can also be a decorative accent in a bare corner.

- Do you need a huge painting but can't afford the price? Tie-dye a single bed sheet by starting the tie in the very center and then spreading out in ever-widening radii, using dye colors that will work in your room. Mixing dyes can be tricky but rewarding. Staple the sheet on the wall and frame it with thin wood lathe stripping all around, or cut the sheet to a manageable size and stretch it, like an artist's canvas, over a wood frame.

- Make an abstract bas-relief of worn-out kitchen utensils like strainers, small sauce or frying pans, spatulas or cutlery. Glue these to a plywood or Masonite shape—a large circle or square will do nicely—and then spray the whole thing in glossy white paint. This collection will look like a very classy bit of abstract art in your living room.

- Antique kitchen utensils like butter stamps, tongs, old measuring cups or rolling pins were made of wood when metal was not available. When they are polished up, a collection of these utensils makes an elegant table-top sculptural arrangement on a modern clear or white plexiglas tray.

- The kitchen department is a good place to shop for your living room. Earthenware mixing bowls in natural colors can hold fruits or flowers, clear glass cannisters store nuts and candies or cigarettes; and earthenware pitchers make handsome additions to your bar.

- Odd cups and saucers can provide attractive table-top decorations and are useable as well. A whole group of unmatched but elegant demitasse coffee cups and saucers look smashing on a modern glass coffee table or sideboard. You can often buy a single set for very little, and the combined patterns and styles look marvelous together. What's more, you can use them for after-dinner coffee; let each guest choose his or her own favorite.

- Anything on a pedestal tends to look like sculpture. A beautiful basket, a piece of crude primitive sculpture, a large conch shell, even a television set can be given real stature. The pedestal can be small, to suit whatever you want to feature, and can stand on a table, or it can be a tall version, to fill extra space.

- A plant on a pedestal gives height to a room where needed to balance a tall lamp or painting. A luscious fern or flowing grape ivy on a tall white lacquer pedestal does a lot to give height and texture and pattern to any room. The pedestal can also be moved easily, or the plant exchanged for another, if there's not enough sun where you want it.

- Baskets are in vogue today, which is good news for those of us with small budgets. A set of nestling baskets from Thailand, for instance, costs fifteen dollars for a set of five and can be used for jewels to junk, bread to bathsoap, plants to potato chips. Even just empty, baskets can be stacked in a group on a table for sculptural elegance.

- You can still find old shop signs in country antique barns. Eyeglass outlines of worn wood, the bootmaker's boot in painted wood, a handsome large fish from a fishmonger of yesterday—all make instant, unique and genuine works of art in the contemporary living room.

About the Author

EMILY MALINO, A.S.I.D. (American Society of Interior Designers) has been recognized as one of the ten most influential American designers by the prestigious *Interiors* magazine, and she is a former vice-president of the Architectural League. With offices in New York City and Washington, D.C., she has designed homes and offices for celebrities in politics, business and theater. Her nationally syndicated column "Design for People" is featured in such newspapers as the *Washington Post, Boston Globe, Houston Chronicle* and many others. She has written for all the leading home and design magazines and lectures widely across the country. In private life Emily Malino is the wife of Congressman James H. Scheuer and the mother of two girls and two boys.